LiMUR SHIFMAN

The MIT Press | Cambridge, Massachusetts | London, England

© 2014 Massachusetts Institute of Technology

All rights reserved. No part of this book may be reproduced in any form by any electronic or mechanical means (including photocopying, recording, or information storage and retrieval) without permission in writing from the publisher.

MIT Press books may be purchased at special quantity discounts for business or sales promotional use. For information, please email special_sales@ mitpress.mit.edu.

This book was set in Chaparral Pro by the MIT Press. Printed and bound in the United States of America.

Library of Congress Cataloging-in-Publication Data

Shifman, Limor, 1974–.
Memes in Digital Culture/ Limor Shifman.
    pages   cm.—(MIT press essential knowledge)
Includes bibliographical references and index.
ISBN 978-0-262-52543-5 (pbk. : alk. paper)
1. Social evolution. 2. Memes. 3. Culture diffusion. 4. Internet—Social aspects. 5. Memetics. I. Title.
HM626.S55   2014
302—dc23
2013012983

10   9   8   7   6

CONTENTS

SERIES FOREWORD

The MIT Press Essential Knowledge series offers accessible, concise, beautifully produced pocket-size books on topics of current interest. Written by leading thinkers, the books in this series deliver expert overviews of subjects that range from the cultural and the historical to the scientific and the technical.

In today's era of instant information gratification, we have ready access to opinions, rationalizations, and superficial descriptions. Much harder to come by is the foundational knowledge that informs a principled understanding of the world. Essential Knowledge books fill that need. Synthesizing specialized subject matter for nonspecialists and engaging critical topics through fundamentals, each of these compact volumes offers readers a point of access to complex ideas.

Bruce Tidor
Professor of Biological Engineering and Computer Science
Massachusetts Institute of Technology

ACKNOWLEDGMENTS

This book could not have been written without the support of a number of patient colleagues who have put up with my meme obsession over the last few years. I am indebted to Elad Segev, Paul Frosh, Ben Peters, Nicholas John, and Leora Hadas for their valuable comments on parts of this manuscript. I am particularly grateful to Menahem Blondheim, the most generous friend and intellectual I have ever encountered.

I consider myself extremely fortunate to be part of the Department of Communication at the Hebrew University of Jerusalem. I have benefited greatly from the wisdom and kindness of my friends in this wonderful academic home. Besides those mentioned above, other colleagues and graduate students from the department—in particular Elihu Katz, Zohar Kampf, Keren Tenenboim-Weinblatt, Asaf Nissenboim, Noam Gal, and Lillian Boxman-Shabtai—offered many insightful observations and criticisms. The members of the "Jerusalem Discourse Forum"—Gonen Hacohen, Michal Hamo, Ayelet Kohn, Chaim Noy, and Motti Neiger—raised enlightening issues in two brainstorming sessions dedicated to memes.

I started my journey to the light heavyweight side of the Internet as a postdoctoral researcher at the Oxford Internet Institute, UK. My colleagues at the Institute, particularly Bill Dutton and Stephen Coleman, fully backed my plan to study the (then) eccentric topic of Internet humor. I am also extremely grateful to danah boyd and Nancy Baym from Microsoft Research. Their ongoing support means a lot to me.

Parts of the introduction and chapters 2, 3, 4, and 6 were originally published in the *Journal of Computer-Mediated Communication* ("Memes in a Digital World: Reconciling with a Conceptual Troublemaker," 2013, 18[3]) and *New Media & Society* ("An Anatomy of a YouTube Meme," 2012, 14[2]). I am thankful to the editors and publishers of those journals for their assistance and permission to reuse the papers.

My gratitude also goes to the editorial and production staff at MIT Press, particularly Margy Avery, who supported this project enthusiastically even before I knew that I wanted to write a book, and Judith Feldmann, who edited it with great sensitivity. Three anonymous reviewers offered thoughtful, constructive, and wise comments on the manuscript, and I'm greatly appreciative of that.

Finally, I wish to thank my parents, Nili and Tommy Schoenfeld, my husband, Sagiv, and my children, Neta and Yuval. My love and gratitude is beyond what any meme could express.

INTRODUCTION

On December 21, 2012, a somewhat peculiar video broke YouTube's all-time viewing records. Performed by a South Korean singer named PSY, "Gangnam Style" was the first clip to surpass the one-billion-view mark. But the Gangnam phenomenon was not only a tale of sheer popularity. Besides watching the clip, people also responded to it creatively, in dazzling volume. Internet users from places as far-flung as Indonesia and Spain, Russia and Israel, the United States and Saudi Arabia imitated the horse-riding dance from the original video while replacing the reference to Gangnam—a luxurious neighborhood in Seoul—with local settings and protagonists, generating videos such as "Mitt Romney Style," "Singaporean Style," and "Arab Style." At first glance, this whole process seems enigmatic. How did such a bizarre piece of culture become so successful? Why are so many people investing so much effort in imitating it? And why do some of these amateur imitations attract millions of viewers? In what follows, I suggest that the key to these questions lies in defining "Gangnam Style"—as well as many other similar Internet phenomena—as an *Internet meme.*

The term "meme" was coined by Richard Dawkins in 1976 to describe small units of culture that spread from person to person by copying or imitation. Since then, the meme concept has been the subject of constant academic debate, derision, and even outright dismissal. Recently, however, the term once kicked out the door by many academics is coming back through the Windows (and other operating systems) of Internet users. In the vernacular discourse of netizens, the tag "Internet meme" is commonly applied to describe the propagation of items such as jokes, rumors, videos, and websites from person to person via the Internet. As illustrated by the Gangnam Style case, a central attribute of Internet memes is their sparking of user-created derivatives articulated as parodies, remixes, or mashups. "Leave Britney Alone," "*Star Wars* Kid," "*Hitler's Downfall* Parodies," "Nyan Cat," and the "Situation Room" Photoshops are particularly famous drops in a memetic ocean.

Another fundamental attribute of Internet memes is intertextuality: memes often relate to each other in complex, creative, and surprising ways. The example in figure 1 demonstrates such an amalgamate between "Gangnam Style" and "Binders Full of Women"—a meme created in

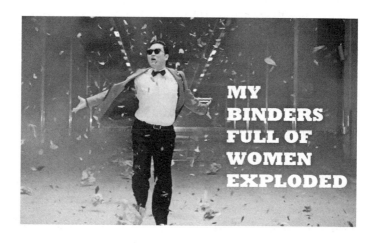

Figure 1 When "Gangnam Style" meets "Binders Full of Women." Source: http://bindersfullofwomen.tumblr.com/.

response to an assertion made by Mitt Romney in a 2012 US presidential debate about the "binders full of women" that he asked for in order to locate female job applicants for senior positions. While an eccentric Korean rapper might seem as far as one may get from an affluent American presidential candidate, meme creators managed to link them. "My Binders Full of Women Exploded" is thus not only a striking example of intertextuality; it also demonstrates that this new arena of bottom-up expression can blend pop culture, politics, and participation in unexpected ways.

This book is a first step in bridging the yawning gap between (skeptic) academic and (enthusiastic) popular discourse about memes. Internet users are on to something, and researchers should follow. Users seem to have sensed that the meme concept encapsulates some of the most fundamental aspects of contemporary digital culture. Like many Web 2.0 applications, memes diffuse from person to person, but shape and reflect general social mindsets. The term describes cultural reproduction as driven by various means of copying and imitation—practices that have become essential in contemporary digital culture. In this environment, user-driven imitation and remixing are not just prevalent practices: they have become highly valued pillars of a so-called *participatory culture*. In what follows, I will argue that we live in an era driven by a *hypermemetic* logic, in which almost every major public event sprouts a stream of memes. In this sense, Internet memes are like Forrest

Like many Web 2.0 applications, memes diffuse from person to person, but shape and reflect general social mindsets.

Gump. Ostensibly, they are trivial pieces of pop culture; yet, a deeper look reveals that they play an integral part in some of the defining events of the twenty-first century.

In what follows, I explore the utility of memes for understanding digital culture, positing two premises throughout. First, the intense emotions and dramatic statements characterizing both sides of the memes debate need to be toned down. While enthusiastic advocates argue that the meme concept explains everything and their opponents assert that it explains and changes absolutely nothing, it might be worth asking whether the term may be useful for *something*. Here I follow in the footsteps of researchers such as Michele Knobel, Colin Lankshear, Lance Bennett, Ryan Milner, and Jean Burgess, who have used the meme as a prism for understanding certain aspects of contemporary culture without embracing the whole set of implications and meanings ascribed to it over the years.

My second assertion is that we should look at memes from a communication-oriented perspective. Coined by a biologist, the term "meme" has been widely adopted (and disputed) in many disciplines, including psychology, philosophy, anthropology, folklore, and linguistics. For the most part, however, it has been utterly ignored in the field of communication. Until the twenty-first century, mass communication researchers felt comfortable overlooking memes. As units that propagate *gradually* through many interpersonal contacts, memes were considered irrelevant for understanding mass-mediated content, which is often transmitted simultaneously from a single institutional source to many people. But this is no longer the case in an era of blurring boundaries between interpersonal and mass, professional and amateur, bottom-up and top-down communications. In a time marked by a convergence of media platforms, when content flows swiftly from one medium to another, memes have become more relevant than ever to communication scholarship.

While memes and digital culture seem like a match made in heaven, several issues need to be resolved before the concept can be integrated meaningfully into academia and industry. First, there is a core problem about the exact meaning of the term—the jury is still out on what is meant by "meme." Second, many competing terms—such as "viral"—tend to be used interchangeably with it. And finally, only a handful of studies have actually examined the practices and politics involved in the creation and diffusion of Internet memes.

And that is where this book comes in. In its first part, I survey the history of the term "meme" (chapter 2), tracing the controversies associated with the concept as well as its renaissance in the digital age (chapter 3). I then introduce a new definition for Internet memes (chapter 4). Instead of depicting the meme as a single cultural unit that has propagated successfully, I suggest defining an Internet meme as (a) a *group of digital items sharing common characteristics* of content, form, and/or stance; (b) that were created *with awareness of each other*; and (c) were circulated, imitated, and/or transformed *via the Internet by many users*. This definition is helpful for analyzing Internet memes as *socially constructed public discourses* in which different memetic variants represent diverse voices and perspectives. In chapter 5, I differentiate between Internet memes and virals. While these concepts are often used interchangeably, charting the differences between them enables us to better understand what's going on in the ostensibly chaotic world of user-generated content. This differentiation between memes and virals sets the basis for chapter 6, in which I address the question of success, comparing features characterizing viral and memetic "hits." The rest of the book is devoted almost solely to Internet memes (rather than virals), covering three dimensions: popular meme genres (chapter 7), the political role of memes in democratic and nondemocratic contexts (chapter 8), and memes as globalizing agents (chapter 9). This book was written—and should be read—as a primer for the study of Internet memes. As such, it introduces some core definitions, controversies, and research trajectories, but it does not offer an in-depth contextual analysis of all the memes mentioned. In the final section of the book (chapter 10), I present some possible paths of future research that may help others in conducting such in-depth analyses.

A TELEGRAPHIC BIOGRAPHY OF A CONCEPTUAL TROUBLEMAKER

The term "meme" was introduced by the biologist Richard Dawkins in his 1976 book *The Selfish Gene*. As part of his larger effort to apply evolutionary theory to cultural change, Dawkins defined memes as small cultural units of transmission, analogous to genes, that spread from person to person by copying or imitation. Examples of memes in his pioneering essay include cultural artifacts such as melodies, catchphrases, and clothing fashions, as well as abstract beliefs (for instance, the concept of God). Like genes, memes are defined as replicators that undergo variation, competition, selection, and retention. At any given moment, many memes are competing for the attention of hosts; however, only memes suited to their sociocultural environment spread successfully, while others become extinct. Dawkins also noted that certain groups of coadaptive memes tend to be replicated together—strengthening each other in the process. Dawkins called such groups "coadapted meme complexes," a tag later shortened by Hans-Cees Speel to "memeplexes."[1] Democracy, for instance, can be regarded as a memeplex that includes several submemeplexes such as human rights and free regular elections, which can further be broken down to respective memes.

The word "meme" derives from the Greek *mimema*, signifying "something which is imitated," which Dawkins shortened to rhyme with "gene." Interestingly, a similar term to signify cultural evolution had appeared a century earlier. In 1870 the Austrian sociologist Ewald Hering coined the term "die Mneme" (from the Greek *mneme*, meaning memory), which the German biologist Richard Semon used in the title of a book he published in 1904. Unaware of this existing terminology, Dawkins's expression proved an accidental but successful imitation in itself: his concept survived and proliferated in the scientific world.[2]

After more than a decade of sporadic growth, *memetics*—described by Francis Heylighen and Klaas Chielens[3] as "the theoretical and empirical science that studies the replication, spread and evolution of memes"—began to take shape as an active research program, drawing scientists from many fields in the 1990s. Important landmarks on this path included contributions from the prominent philosophers Douglas Hofstadter and Daniel C. Dennett, the emergence of the *Journal of Memetics* in 1997 and its publication until 2005, and the publication of several meme-oriented books. Of these, Susan Blackmore's *The Meme Machine* from 1999 may well be the most influential, yet also the most disputed.

Since its early days, memetics has drawn constant fire. Two controversies surrounding memes—tagged as "biological analogies" and "who's the boss"—are particularly relevant to the topic of this book. The "biological analogies" dispute relates to the strong tendency to liken memes to both viruses and genes. The meme-as-virus analogy sees a similarity between memes and disease agents. Taking *epidemiology* as its model, it considers memes as the cultural equivalents of flu bacilli, transmitted through the communicational equivalents of sneezes. In Internet culture, this metaphor is prevalent in the highly visible discourse on viral content. Yet Henry Jenkins and his colleagues rightfully assert that this metaphor has been used in a problematic way, conceptualizing people as helpless and passive creatures, susceptible to the domination of meaningless media "snacks" that infect their minds.[4]

The second prevalent biological metaphor for memes—derived directly from Dawkins's work—takes *evolutionary genetics* as its model. However, some works have taken this analogy too far, seeking cultural equivalents for all principal evolutionary genetic concepts, including genotype, phenotype, transcription, and code. This effort was criticized not only because memes behave very differently than genes, but also because reducing culture to biology narrows and simplifies complex human behaviors. The prevalent notion is thus that the meme–gene analogy should be taken with many grains of salt. Indeed, it is not necessary to think of biology when analyzing memes. The ideas of replication, adaptation, and fitness to a certain environment can be analyzed from a purely sociocultural perspective.

The second fundamental controversy in memetics, tagged here as "who's the boss," relates to the issue of human agency in the process of meme diffusion. At one end of the spectrum are scholars such as Susan Blackmore, who claims in *The Meme Machine* that people are merely devices operated by the numerous memes they host and constantly spread. I contend, on the other hand, that the undermining of human agency is inherent not to the meme concept itself, but only to one strain of its interpretation. A number of works within the field of memetics are clearly opposed to it. Most important to this book is Rosaria Conte's suggestion to treat people not as *vectors* of cultural transmission, but as *actors* behind this process.[5] The dissemination of memes, she submits, is based on intentional agents with decision-making powers: social norms, perceptions, and preferences are crucial in memetic selection processes. As I will elaborate in chapter 3, the depiction of people as active agents is essential for understanding Internet memes, particularly when meaning is dramatically altered in the course of memetic diffusion.

While widely disputed in academia, the meme concept has been enthusiastically picked up by Internet users. A search of Google Trends suggests a spurt of interest on the subject since 2011, and a recent Google query of the term "Internet meme" yielded around 1,900,000 hits, many of them leading to large interactive meme depositories. For example, on the popular website Know Your Meme (http://knowyourmeme.com), "resident internet scientists" appropriately dressed in white coats provide various explanations for certain memes' success. At other popular "meme hubs"—such as 4chan, Reddit, and Tumblr—a constant flow of Internet memes is uploaded and negotiated daily. According to Michele Knobel and Koline Lankshear, Internet users employ the word "meme" to describe the rapid uptake and spread of a "particular idea presented as a written text, image, language 'move,' or some other unit of cultural 'stuff.'"[6] This vernacular use of the term, the authors submit, differs utterly from its use in the academic study of memetics: if the former tends to describe recent, often short-lasting fads, longevity is the key to "serious" memetics, since successful memes are defined as the ones that survive in the long term.

Another difference relates to the object of analysis: whereas in memetics the unit of analysis itself is abstract and controversial, Internet users tend to ascribe the meme tag to observable audiovisual content, such as YouTube videos and humorous images. But the gap between the

Internet memes can be treated as (post)modern folklore, in which shared norms and values are constructed through cultural artifacts such as Photoshopped images or urban legends.

popular and serious accounts of memes can be bridged. While memes are seemingly trivial and mundane artifacts, they actually reflect deep social and cultural structures. In many senses, Internet memes can be treated as (post)modern folklore, in which shared norms and values are constructed through cultural artifacts such as Photoshopped images or urban legends.[7] For instance, in chapter 8 I show how postfeminist ideas about gender differences are circulated globally through Internet jokes, and how critical approaches toward race-based stereotyping are reflected in visual memes. Whereas a single meme may rise and fall as quick as a flash, revealing the common ideas and forms shared by *many* Internet memes might tell us something about digital culture. For instance, while the single lipdub "Numa Numa" features one guy from New Jersey, its analysis in chapter 7 as part of a stream of thousands of similar videos that constitute the lipdub genre will reveal a larger story about the eroding boundaries between top-down pop culture and bottom-up folk culture in contemporary society. Moreover, as I will demonstrate in the next chapter, the meme concept is not only useful for understanding cultural trends: it epitomizes the very essence of the so-called Web 2.0 era.

WHEN MEMES GO DIGITAL

The uptick in vibrant popular discourse about memes in an era increasingly defined by digital communication is not coincidental. Although the term "meme" was coined long before the digital era, the Internet's unique features turned memes' diffusion into a ubiquitous and highly visible routine. According to Dawkins's analysis in *The Selfish Gene*, memes that spread successfully incorporate three basic properties—*longevity*, *fecundity*, and *copy fidelity*. All three are enhanced by the Internet. Online meme transmission has higher copy fidelity (that is, accuracy) than communication through other media, since digitization allows lossless information transfer. Fecundity (the number of copies made in a time unit) is also greatly increased— the Internet facilitates the swift diffusion of any given message to numerous nodes. Longevity may potentially increase, as well, because information can be stored indefinitely in numerous archives.[1]

Yet the scale, scope, and accuracy of digital meme diffusion are only the tips of the iceberg with regard to the meme–Internet congruence. What Internet users seemed to have grasped—and Richard Dawkins couldn't have imagined back in 1976—is that *the meme is the best concept to encapsulate some of the most fundamental aspects of the Internet* in general, and of the so-called participatory or Web 2.0 culture in particular. Three main attributes ascribed to memes are particularly relevant to the analysis of contemporary digital culture: (1) a gradual propagation from individuals to society, (2) reproduction via copying and imitation, and (3) diffusion through competition and selection.

First, memes may best be understood as pieces of *cultural information that pass along from person to person, but gradually scale into a shared social phenomenon*. Although they spread on a micro basis, their impact is on the macro level: memes shape the mindsets, forms of behavior, and actions of social groups. This attribute is highly compatible to the way culture is formed in the Web 2.0 era, which is marked by platforms for creating and exchanging user-generated content. YouTube, Twitter, Facebook, Wikipedia, and other similar applications and sites are based on propagation of content, to paraphrase Abraham Lincoln, of the users, by the users, and for the users. Such sites represent "express paths" for meme diffusion: content spread by individuals through their social networks can scale up to mass levels within hours.

Moreover, the basic activity of spreading memes has become desired and highly valued, as it is associated with what Nicholas John has identified as the constitutive activity of Web 2.0: *sharing*. John's historical analysis shows that since 2007, "sharing" has become the overarching term to describe a variety of activities such as uploading photographs, updating a Facebook status, Tweeting, or posting a review on Amazon. Yet sharing is not only a buzzword: it has emerged as a central cultural logic, encompassing realms such as "sharing economies" and sharing emotions in intimate relationships. In this new era, the two meanings of the term in the predigital age—sharing as distribution and sharing as communication—converge. When I post a funny clip on Facebook, I distribute a cultural item and at the same time express my feelings about it. And most often, I anticipate that others will continue spreading the piece that I have enjoyed so much. In other words: sharing content—or spreading memes—is now a fundamental part of what participants experience as the digital sphere.[2]

A second attribute of memes is that they reproduce by *various means of repackaging* or *imitation*. In oral communication, people become aware of memes through their senses, process them in their minds, and then "repackage" them in order to pass them along to others. In this process, memes often change their form and content—it is almost impossible to retell a joke using the exact words in which it was originally uttered. In the digital age, however, people do not have to repackage memes: they can spread content *as is* by forwarding, linking, or copying. Yet a quick look at any Web 2.0 environment reveals that people do choose to create their *own versions* of Internet memes, and in startling volumes.

Two main repackaging mechanisms of memes are prevalent on the Web: *mimicry* and *remix*. Mimicry involves the practice of "redoing"—the re-creation of a specific text by other people and/or by other means. In its essence, mimicry is not new—people have always engaged in impersonating others—whether these were domineering parents, annoying teachers, or hypocrite politicians. In fact, imitation is what has stood, according to Blackmore, at the very basis of meme diffusion since the dawn of humanity. However, in the Web 2.0 era, everyday mimetic praxis has turned into a highly visible phenomenon in the public sphere. On websites such as YouTube, almost any user-generated video that passes a certain view threshold inspires a stream of emulations. Figure 2 features one of these highly mimicked videos— the clip "Charlie Bit My Finger," started by two English brothers, Harry and Charlie Davies-Carr. Yet mimicry is relevant not only to video; in the case of mimetic still

Figure 2 Various means of imitation: "Charlie Bit My Finger" imitated and remixed. Source: http://www.youtube.com.

Original

Remix

Mimicry

images, it takes the form of reconstructing images in Lego, dough, or Simpsons characters.

The second strategy of digital meme repackaging, *remixing*, is a newer one. It involves technology-based manipulation, for instance by Photoshopping an image or adding a new soundtrack. A plethora of user-friendly applications that enable people to download and re-edit content have turned remixing into an extremely popular practice. Mimicry and remix are thus conquering the Web, and the term "meme" seems particularly suitable to describe this glut of reworks, as the concept—deliberately connoting "mimesis"—is flexible enough to capture a wide range of communicative intentions and actions, spanning all the way from naive copying to scornful imitation.

A third attribute of memes that is amplified in digital environments is their diffusion through *competition* and *selection*. Memes vary greatly in their degree of fitness, that is, their adaptability to the sociocultural environment in which they propagate. Although processes of cultural selection are ancient, digital media have afforded researchers the ability to *trace* the spread and evolution of memes. And it is not only experts who can now analyze digital traces on the Web—on many Web 2.0–friendly websites, metadata about viewing preferences, choices, and responses is constantly aggregated and displayed for all users. Thus, meta-information about competition and selection processes is increasingly becoming a visible and influential part of the process itself—people take it into consideration before they decide to download an album, remake a video, or even march in a street protest.

In this section, I've demonstrated how three features ascribed to memes—micro–macro propagation, replication through imitation, and selective competition—are strongly manifest in digital environments. Yet these qualities are not just amplified in the digital era. In the last few years, sharing, imitating, remixing, and using popularity measurements have become highly valued pillars of participatory culture, part and parcel of what is expected from a "digitally literate" netizen. This new environment is dominated by what I call a *hypermemetic logic*. "Hyper" refers not only to the fact that memes spread more widely and swiftly than ever before, but also to their evolution as a new vernacular that permeates many spheres of digital and nondigital expression.

This pervasiveness of Internet memes becomes evident when they appear in unexpected circumstances, such as the ostensibly private occasion of a marriage proposal. In November 2011, a young blogger named Timothy Tiah Ewe Tiam approached his girlfriend in a restaurant and began showing her poster-sized printed memes, accompanied with his own captions. Finally, he got to the point (see figure 3). A video featuring the proposal and the (positive) reaction to it was then uploaded to YouTube and other social media platforms, sparking memetic responses in the form of other meme-based marriage proposals. In this case and others, "hypermemetic" assumes a further meaning: it depicts a culture in which memes have a multidimensional presence.

The hypermemetic nature of contemporary culture can be further clarified by a comparison between "old" and "new" memes. As I note above, memes were not born with the Internet; they were always part of human society. However, I argue that the digital era did change some fundamental aspects of memes. To demonstrate this, I will take a close look at one veteran meme: "Kilroy Was Here." This meme incorporated a simple drawing of a man with a long nose looking over a wall, alongside a mysterious caption: "Kilroy Was Here." It was launched during World War II, and though its origins are still a matter of debate, the most agreed-upon version, according to Daniel Gilmore, links it to a Massachusetts shipyard inspector named James J. Kilroy.[3] Kilroy's job was to examine riveters' work after they completed their shifts. To keep track of his inspections, he began marking inspected areas with the phrase "Kilroy Was Here." When the ships were completed and launched to the battlefield, soldiers noticed these scribblings. Kilroy appeared everywhere, even in the weirdest and most unexpected internal parts of the ships. Soldiers began to inscribe the slogan on diverse surfaces, and at some point they added a drawing of a little man with a big nose. A meme was born. Throughout the

Figure 3 A meme-based marriage proposal. Source: http://ryanseacrest.com/.

war, the doodle popped up in almost any imaginable space within the reach of Allied soldiers, who then brought it back to the United States (and other countries). After the war, Kilroy was reincarnated in urban graffiti, as well as in various pop-culture artifacts.

Henrik Bjarneskans, Bjarne Grønnevik, and Anders Sandberg have analyzed Kilroy's memetic success.[4] In addition to the fact that the message was simple and could thus be easily reproduced, it also tended to appear in public places, which ensured that many people, or "potential hosts" who could further diffuse the meme, noticed it. That the slogan's "real" meaning was mysterious and open to interpretation was also an advantage, as it allowed each person to endow it with his or her own preferred meaning. Moreover, this lack of obvious meaning made the meme hard to contradict and, at the same time, enhanced people's engagement with it as they tried to solve the mystery. When attempting to decipher what motivated people to replicate the meme with no direct incentive in the form of peer-reaction, Bjarneskans and his colleagues postulate that people strove to join a circle of individuals who "shared the joke." In this way, the act of reproducing the meme created an invisible bond with a community of "Kilroy writers," or a sense of membership in a privileged and

Figure 4   "Kilroy Was Here." Source: http://commons.wikimedia.org/wiki/Category:Kilroy_was_here.

mysterious brotherhood. At first glance, "Kilroy Was Here" seems surprisingly similar to some contemporary Internet memes. For instance, it shares many features with "planking," which basically involves people lying face down with their arms at their sides in public places (see figure 5), or "241543903/Heads in Freezers," in which people are photographed with their heads in a freezer and post the photos tagged with the number 241543903, allowing easy detection via search engines. Like "Kilroy Was Here," these instances involve bizarre, weird, and unexpected juxtapositions. Moreover, in all three memes, people imitate a certain action in a unique setting and form a bond with those "in the know." And finally, they are all imbedded in the "real" (that is, outside of the Internet) world.

Yet beyond these commonalities, traditional and Internet-based memes differ in several fundamental ways. The first distinction relates to individuals' awareness of the overall meme-scape. In the pre-Internet era, each individual was exposed to a very limited number of memetic manifestations—a person might have seen the Kilroy graffiti a dozen times in his or her lifetime, but probably not much more than that. Since the main realm in which the meme existed was the streets, its true magnitude was

Figure 5 The planking meme. Sources: http://ourtwobits.com/ a-perspective-on-planking-the-evolution-of-a-revolution/; http://www .squidoo.com/planking-whats-wrong-with-people.

always a mystery. By contrast, the "real world" existence of memes like planking is often ephemeral, as they are based on capturing a moment through photography. Yet the corpus as a whole is very much alive on the Web: it only takes a couple of mouse clicks to see hundreds of versions of the planking or head in the freezer memes. If with Kilroy and its ilk most variants were invisible to most participants, the visibility of memetic variability—as well as the timeline of the memes' appearance—is an integral part of contemporary Internet memes. This is another aspect of what I term the hypermemetic: memes are present in the public and private sphere not as sporadic entities but as monstrously sized groups of texts and images.

A further difference between Internet and traditional memes relates to the central place of the meme's creator in the former. In particular, memetic videos and photos often focus much more on the performative self. Uploaders become both the meme's medium and its message: their faces and/or bodies are integral parts of it. Thus, such memes are emblems of a culture saturated with personal branding and strategic self-commodification.[5] As I will elaborate in the next section, this attribute aligns with a common social logic: in an era marked by "network individualism," people use memes to simultaneously express both their uniqueness and their connectivity.

In an era marked by "network individualism," people use memes to simultaneously express both their uniqueness and their connectivity.

Probing "Hypermemetic Logic"

So far, I have *described* the compatibility between memes and contemporary digital culture. Now I shall try to *explain* it. Why are so many people driven to re-create videos and images that others have produced? What are the potential benefits of such an activity, and for whom? While a full explanation of contemporary hypermemetic logic falls beyond the scope of a single book (particularly a short one), to spark the discussion I will suggest three initial prisms for understanding it, rooted in economic, social, and cultural logics of participation.

The *economy*-driven logic relates to the notion that contemporary society is based on an "attention economy."[6] Whereas the old economic system focused on things, the most valuable resource in the information era is not information but the attention people pay to it. On sites such as YouTube, attention can be directly tied to mimesis: the number of derivatives spawned by a certain video is an indicator of attention, which, in turn, draws attention to the initial memetic video in a reciprocal process. This dynamic is particularly pertinent to user-generated content: whereas attention paid to corporate-produced videos largely relates to the status of mass media stars, attention to an amateur video is not guaranteed—it can, however, be accumulated through mimetic activity. According to this logic, a video structured for easy replication has a chance to succeed in YouTube's attention economy. This logic also applies to those who imitate famous memetic videos: emulations may get attention because they are similar to a successful video, and thus will appear in You-Tube's "suggestions" bar or pop up as a highly relevant search result when one is looking for the "original" video. Using memetic activity to drive attention is also evident in campaigns led by political parties or activists. In such campaigns, the reappropriation of messages (such as "We are the 99 percent") by numerous users helps in promoting a topic on the mass media agenda, which, in turn, draws more attention to it.

The second prism through which we can understand memetic activities is the *social* logic of participation, which can be linked to what Barry Wellman and others describe as "networked individualism." In our era of accelerated in-dividualization, people are expected to fashion a unique identity and image and by doing so actively construct their "selves." At the same time, individuals participate enthusiastically in the shaping of social networks, dem-onstrating an enduring human longing for communality. User-generated versions of an Internet meme may serve as a way to have it all: on the one hand, users who upload a self-made video or a Photoshopped image signify that they are digitally literate, unique, and creative; on the other hand, the text that they upload often relates to a common, widely shared memetic video, image, or formula. By this referencing, users simultaneously indicate and construct their individuality and their affiliation with the larger You-Tube, Tumblr, or 4chan community. Re-creating popular videos and images can thus be seen as the cultural embodiment of "networked individualism": it allows people to be "themselves," together.

The third prism through which the miming phenomena can be examined is based on the *cultural and aesthetic logics of participation.* It draws on the notion that memes are not confined to the secluded spheres of YouTube or 4chan, or even to the Internet at large. Since memes serve as the building blocks of complex cultures, we need to focus not only on the texts but also on the cultural practices surrounding them. Jean Burgess suggests treating You-Tube videos as mediating ideas that are practiced within social networks, shaped by cultural norms and expectations. Such norms are often rooted in the history of pop-culture genres and fan cultures: music videos, for instance, are replicated as part of broader cultures of jamming, remix, and covers that characterize music making.[7] These examples of historical roots highlight the ways in which practices of re-creating videos and images blur the lines between private and public, professional and amateur, market- and non-market-driven activities. Thus, Internet memes can be seen as sites in which historical modes of cultural production meet the new affordances of Web 2.0.

The analysis so far presents memes and digital culture as a match made in heaven: the Internet is not only saturated with memes, but also allows for their investigation in unprecedented ways. However, some controversies surrounding memes—in particular those I referred to in chapter 2 as "biological analogies" and "who's the boss"—have hindered the wide uptake of the concept in studying digital culture. I suggested two paths to overcoming these barriers: forsaking the aspiration to find biological equivalents to all things cultural and ascribing greater agency to humans. In the next chapter, I address a third dispute that obstructs the empirical study of memes: the disagreement on the seemingly simple question, "What is a meme?"

DEFINING INTERNET MEMES

A core problem of memetics, maybe *the* core quandary, is the exact meaning of the term "meme." As mentioned above, Dawkins's initial definition was quite ambiguous: he referred to a meme as "a unit of cultural transmission, or a unit of imitation." His set of meme examples spanned ideas (God), texts (nursery rhymes and jokes), and practices (Christian rituals). Ever since, the study of memes has been subject to disputes centering on the mind–body or genotype–phenotype dichotomy, yielding three positions regarding the nature of memes: mentalist driven, behavior driven, and inclusive.

Mentalist-driven memetics, advocated by leading scholars in the field such as Dawkins himself (in his 1982 clarification of the theory), Daniel Dennett, and Aaron Lynch, is based on the differentiation between memes and meme vehicles. According to this school of thought, memes are ideas or pieces of information that reside in the brain. They are not simple ideas such as *red*, *round*, or *cold*, but complex ones such as ideas of the alphabet, chess, or impressionism.[1] In order to be passed along from one person to another, memes are "loaded" on various vehicles: images, texts, artifacts, or rituals. According to this view, those observable meme vehicles are equivalent to phenotypes—the visible manifestation of genes. In other words, memes are idea complexes and meme vehicles are their tangible expressions.

By contrast, *behavior-driven* memetics sees memes as behaviors and artifacts rather than ideas.[2] In the behaviorist model, the meme vehicle and the meme itself are inseparable: the meme has no existence outside the events, practices, and texts in which it appears; that is, it is always experienced as encoded information. Moreover, this approach claims that if memes were indeed only abstract units of information, it would be impossible to disassociate them from their manifestation in the outside world. Defining memes as concrete units enables their evolution and diffusion to be studied empirically. This brand of memetics is closely related to the scholarly approach known as "diffusion studies." Many studies in this rich tradition focus on the diffusion of "innovations," occasionally adopting the term "meme" and the general memetic framework. However, diffusion studies tend to cling to narrow definitions of memes, thus overlooking the concept's complexity and richness. In particular, this tradition tends to look at the diffused units as stable, well-defined entities with clear boundaries.

Whereas members of the mentalist- and behavior-driven schools see memes as either ideas *or* practices, what I tag as the *inclusive memetic approach*, represented by Susan Blackmore in *The Meme Machine*, uses the term "indiscriminately to refer to memetic information in any of its many forms; including ideas, the brain structures that initiate those ideas, the behaviors these brain structures produce, and their versions in books, recipes, maps and written music" (p. 66); that is, any type of information that can be copied by imitation should be called a meme. But this inclusive approach may lack analytical power, as it assembles very different elements under its large conceptual tent.

Reassessing these standpoints, I suggest a different approach to defining memes. This suggestion is based on two rather simple principles: (a) looking at diffused units as incorporating several *memetic dimensions*—namely, several aspects that people may imitate; and (b) understanding memes not as single entities that propagate well, but as *groups of content units* with common characteristics. I will soon demonstrate how these two principles produce a workable definition of Internet memes.

Going back to Dawkins's original idea—that memes are units of imitation—I find it useful to isolate three dimensions of cultural items that people can potentially imitate: content, form, and stance.[3] The first dimension relates mainly to the *content* of a specific text, referencing to both the ideas and the ideologies conveyed by it. The second dimension relates to *form*: this is the physical incarnation of the message, perceived through our senses. It includes both visual/audible dimensions specific to certain texts and the more complex genre-related patterns organizing them (such as lipsynch or animation). While ideas and their expression have been widely discussed in relation to memes the third dimension is presented here for the first time. This dimension—which relates to the information memes convey about their own communication—is labeled here as *stance*. I use "stance" to depict the ways in which addressers position themselves in relation to the text, its linguistic codes, the addressees, and other potential speakers. As with form and content, stance is potentially memetic; when re-creating a text, users can decide to imitate a certain position that they find appealing or use an utterly different discursive orientation.

Since I use stance in this context as a very broad category, I wish to clarify it by breaking it into three subdimensions, drawing on concepts from discourse and media studies: (1) *participation structures*—which delineate who is entitled to participate and how, as described by Susan Phillips; (2) *keying*—the tone and style of communication, as conceptualized by Erving Goffman and further developed by Shoshanna Blum-Kulka and her colleagues; and

(3) *communicative functions*, used according to the typology suggested by Roman Jakobson. Jakobson identified six fundamental functions of human communication: (a) referential communication, which is oriented toward the context, or the "outside world"; (b) emotive, oriented toward the addresser and his or her emotions; (c) conative, oriented toward the addressee and available paths of actions (e.g., imperatives); (d) phatic, which serves to establish, prolong, or discontinue communication; (e) metalingual, which is used to establish mutual agreement on the code (for example, a definition); and (f) poetic, focusing on the aesthetic or artistic beauty of the construction of the message itself.[4]

In addition to this three-dimensional breakdown, I suggest that for *Internet* memes—which are often based on an extensive and swift mutation rate—it may be useful to turn Dawkins's definition on its head by looking at memes not as single ideas or formulas that propagate well, but as *groups* of content items. Combining these two principles, I define an Internet meme as:

(a) a group of digital items sharing common characteristics of content, form, and/or stance, which (b) were created with awareness of each other, and (c) were circulated, imitated, and/or transformed via the Internet by many users.

This revised definition may help us in providing more nuanced accounts of the meanings and possible implications of Internet memes. To demonstrate its applicability and utility, I will now take a closer look at three memes: "Leave Britney Alone," "It Gets Better," and the "Pepper-Spraying Cop."

Leave Britney (and the Pepper-Spraying Cop?) Alone, It Doesn't Get Better

On September 10, 2007, a young gay blogger and actor named Chris Crocker uploaded a YouTube video in which he reacted to the harsh criticism that followed pop star Britney Spears's lackluster performance on the MTV Music Video Awards. Crying and shouting throughout most of the clip, Crocker implored his viewers to "Leave Britney Alone":

> And how fucking dare anyone out there make fun
> of Britney, after all she's been through! She lost
> her aunt, she went through a divorce, she had two
> fucking kids, her husband turned out to be a user,
> a cheater, and now she's going through a custody
> battle. All you people care about is readers and
> making money off of her. SHE'S A HUMAN! [...] Her
> song is called "give me more" for a reason because
> all you people want is MORE, MORE, MORE, MORE,

MORE! LEAVE HER ALONE! You're lucky she even performed for you BASTARDS! LEAVE BRITNEY ALONE! [...] Leave Britney Spears alone right NOW!

The video gained over two million views within twenty-four hours, and many more in the following days and months. The Crocker sensation was reported on various mainstream media platforms and generated worldwide attention. The video soon spawned a stream of derivatives: mimcry-based clips (in which known actors and ordinary users impersonated Crocker) as well as remix-based clips (in which music, graphic elements, or dubbing were re-edited with the original).

In exploring "Leave Britney Alone" as a meme, we need to examine the distribution of the original video, but perhaps more importantly, we should investigate the structure and meaning of this video's *new variations.* People may *share* a certain video with others for many different reasons (which I will explore in chapter 6), but when they create their *own versions* of it, they inevitably reveal their personal interpretations. Thinking of Internet memes as trinities of content, form, and stance requires that we determine whether the imitator embraces or rejects each of these memetic dimensions. In what follows, I will implement this strategy to evaluate the ways in which Crocker's video was transformed in the course of its memetic diffusion.

Crocker's 2007 video is a complex amalgam of ideas, textual practices, and communicative strategies. Our starting point is the video's content, namely, the ideas and ideologies that it conveys. The text includes, among other things, facts about Britney Spears's life (for example, her two children) and the castigation of people criticizing fallen celebrities. More broadly, in this and other videos, Crocker wishes to convey the message that being gay and effeminate is a legitimate practice. In terms of form, or textual construction, the video's layout features one talking head, filmed in close-up and in one-shot and situated in front of a white cloth. It further features repetitions of certain phrases, raised voice pitch, tears, and distraught hair-hand gestures. The most complex dimension in Crocker's video relates to stance. Regarding the subdimension of *participation structure*, the video, by virtue of its existence, reminds the viewer that a gay, overtly effeminate individual is openly expressing his opinion in the public sphere. *Keying*, as noted above, is the tone, or modality, of the internal framing of discursive events as formed by their participants. People can key their communication as funny, ironic, mocking, pretend, or serious. In the case of "Leave Britney Alone," Crocker keys his utterances as extremely serious and as ultra-emotional—sometimes so serious that, at a remove, it can even appear comical and ambiguously parodic. While some commentators questioned the sincerity of the video, Crocker insisted it was utterly genuine. In relation to the communication functions defined by Jakobson, of the six described above, the most prominent are the referential (Crocker provides us with facts about Britney's life); the conative (viewers are implored to change their behavior); and above all, the emotive, as this video is all about the addresser and his emotional state. In addition, a contextual examination of this video may lead to the identification of a certain phatic function to it. "Leave Britney Alone" is one of a stream of videos uploaded by Crocker on his YouTube channel. Through these frequent feeds, Crocker aspires to maintain the communicative path between himself, his budding acting career, and his faithful YouTube (and MySpace) viewers.[5]

So far, I have charted the memetic dimensions embedded in Crocker's initial video. The question to be addressed now is: Which of these dimensions was imitated with accuracy by Internet users in their derivatives, and which were altered? In other words, which of these dimensions succeeded in the competitive meme selection process? Since it is virtually impossible to track and examine all of this meme's versions, I compiled a sample of twenty highly viewed derivative videos. To create the sample, two queries were used in YouTube's internal search engine: the string "Leave Britney Alone," and the words "leave," "alone," and "Crocker." I then sorted the results according to their view count, and selected the twenty most-viewed videos (above 100,000) in which people imitate Crocker. Analyzing them qualitatively, I aimed at identifying patterns of memetic uptake.

Among the three memetic dimensions, the one that viewers imitated with a high level of accuracy is the video's form. The mise-en-scène of one person in front of a white cloth filmed in one-shot was evident in virtually all texts. Men were featured in sixteen videos out of twenty, often bearing feminine markers similar to Crocker's (such as a wig or eyeliner). In addition, the composition style of Crocker's sentences was repeated throughout the sample, as were key phrases such as "leave X alone" and "she/he is a human."

In contrast to the relative accuracy in the imitation of the videos' form, radical changes take place on both the content and stance dimensions. These alternations are related, to a large extent, to the construction of *all* the videos in the sample as *parodies*. A major feature of parody is its critical stance vis-à-vis the source text that it mimics. While all parody includes some kind of imitation, it is important to note that not all imitations are parodies. Many YouTube videos are emulated without mocking their protagonists. For instance, the "Evolution of Dance" hit—itself capturing an openly self-parodying event—has spawned numerous imitations in which people copy the performer's dance movements in various contexts, without lampooning him. This is distinctly not the case in "Leave Britney Alone," where the parodic intentions of the original are at best ambiguous and highly exploitable. As I demonstrate below, parody

While all parody includes some kind of imitation, it is important to note that not all imitations are parodies.

targets both the ideological and communicative aspects of the original meme.

Crocker's message about the legitimacy of being an overtly effeminate homosexual is lampooned in many of the videos. For instance, the comedian Seth Green, in a heavily viewed parody, shouts and "implores" the audience to leave Chris Crocker alone, pausing occasionally to fix his black eyeliner: "You have not spent a mile walking in his sneakers, or, platform pumps ... I don't know what he wears ... BUT I BET IT'S STYLISH!" Other clips mock a battery of pop stars and celebrities. In videos such as "Leave Justin Bieber Alone" or "Leave Rebecca Black Alone," the presenters mock Crocker's outcry to pity celebrities by publicly bashing them. Such clips represent a radical alternation of the original video's stance, particularly its *keying* (the tone and style of communication). User-generated derivatives abandon Crocker's overtly emotional performance in favor of a cynical and ironic one. No one says what he or she means in these videos. When a speaker pleads with his audiences to "leave Michael Jackson alone" because he "loves his monkey," it is quite clear that the words spoken are not those meant. Curiously enough, the vast majority of the sampled videos employ common ironic keying: these videos are more similar to *each other* than to Crocker's original.

My analysis so far yields a complex web of imitations and memetic dimensions. While users emulate the forms manifested in Crocker's video, they imitate the other imitators to construct opposing memes at the content and stance dimensions. In other words, the process of imitation combines overt copying and reversing aspects of the original event. It may be that the most powerful communication-oriented meme spread by users in this process is ironic communication: communication that veers from a definite commitment to one's uttered words, using language in a playful and non-obliging way.

In a recent work using the three-dimensional meme model, Noam Gal examined the role of memetic practices in Internet-based collective identity formation.[6] She focused on a participatory YouTube campaign entitled "It Gets Better," produced as a response to vast media coverage of gay teen suicide in the United States as a result of homophobic bullying. Gal analyzed this stream of videos as a meme; people create new versions in response to the former ones, preserving and altering various aspects. Through this practice of partial citation, a distinct discursive arena is constituted, shaped by an ongoing negotiation over its norms and conventions. To investigate the construction of identity through the aggregation of sporadic acts of imitation and deviation, Gal analyzed qualitatively and quantitatively 200 campaign videos. In terms of content, she found that campaign videos tend to describe both the problems of gay teens and their solutions as associated with the private domain. In relation to stance, she found that the majority of protagonists are white, young, able-bodied American men, constituting a typical hegemonic structure of participation, despite the relative absence of formal gatekeepers from the medium. With regard to form, she found that one mise-en-scène—of a protagonist(s) seated in front of a camera—dominates the corpus. This differentiation between content, form, and stance allowed Gal to identify various modes of compliance and subversion in this campaign: whereas in some videos the rather conservative content was paired with a subversive stance (as in the case of a Puerto Rican woman praising Jesus), in others, radical assertions where packed in professional formats that "blocked" further participation.

So far I have demonstrated the utility of the threefold meme typology through video-based examples. I wish to further illustrate its applicability to other formats, such as image and text. To this end, I'll briefly look into the recent example of the "Pepper-Spraying Cop" meme. On November 18, 2011, students from the University of California, Davis, gathered as part of the Occupy Wall Street protest. When they refused police orders to evacuate the area, two officers reacted by pepper-spraying a row of still-sitting students directly in their faces. Shortly after the incident, videos documenting it were uploaded to YouTube, generating uproar against the excessive use of force by American police officers. A photograph in which one of the officers, John Pike, was shown spraying the students quickly evolved into an Internet meme. Users Photoshopped the "Pepper-Spraying Cop" into an endless array of contexts, spanning historical, artistic, and pop-culture-oriented backgrounds.

The plethora of images constituting the "Pepper-Spraying Cop" meme can be analyzed through the model of content, form, and stance. Such an exercise reveals that while most versions share a similar Photoshop-based form, they vary greatly in terms of content. Content-wise, I identified two main groups of meme versions. The first focuses on political contexts: Pike is shown pepper-spraying iconic American symbols such as George Washington crossing the Delaware, the former US presidents on Mount Rushmore, and the Constitution itself, as well as freedom fighters across the globe (in Tiananmen Square, for example). These political versions share a clear idea, namely that the officer brutally violated the basic values of justice and freedom as represented by the protestors. A second group of user-generated images is pop-culture-oriented. In these versions, Pike is pepper-spraying icons such as Snoopy and Marilyn Monroe, as well as a battery of stars identified with other Internet memes, such as "Little Baby Panda" and "Keyboard Cat." Such pop-culture-oriented meme versions are often open to multiple interpretations. In one case, in which Pike is portrayed as spraying Rebecca Black—a widely scorned teen singer and Internet phenomenon— the original meaning of the photo as criticism of Pike

seems to be almost reversed. This differentiation between two types of memetic content can be further associated with stance alternations. For example, the utterly serious keying of the original photograph has been transformed in the process of memetic uptake, which involves explicit playfulness. However, if the keying of politically oriented versions is mainly sardonic, the predominant tone in the pop-culture-oriented ones is amused and humorous.

The analysis of the "Pepper-Spraying Cop" meme according to the three memetic dimensions reveals that, in contrast to the unified uptake pattern characterizing "Leave Britney Alone," other memes might encompass a more divergent mode of diffusion and evolution. Tracing the ways in which they diffuse may prove that the ostensibly chaotic World Wide Web may in fact follow more organized cultural trajectories than meet the eye.

The differentiation between memetic dimensions may also advance our ability to draw borders between Internet memes. If we think of Internet memes as groups of interconnected content units that share common characteristics, we may further posit that such shared features may include content, form, and stance, and various combinations thereof. Therefore, the definition of a certain meme's scope may rely on the dimension through which

Figure 6 The "Pepper-Spraying Cop" meme. Sources: (top) http://www .tumblr.com/tagged/louise+macabitas (photo credit: Louise Macabitas); (middle and lower) http://www.uproxx.com/webculture/.

it is examined. For instance, if our prism is that of content, or ideas, we may argue that the same content can be expressed in a video, a text, or a Photoshop image. In this case, what we define as a particular "Internet meme" will incorporate different forms. Alternatively, we may identify memetic formats, such as image macros or lip synch, that are used for conveying various ideas. I will return to this distinction in the seventh chapter, in which I will define *genres of Internet memes* as intersections between specific themes and formats.

MEMES VERSUS VIRALS

The closest neighbor of the meme concept in both popular and academic discourse is "viral." While many people use the terms interchangeably, I would like to highlight the difference between them. In a recent article, Jeff Hemsley and Robert Mason provide a comprehensive definition of "virality." They describe it as "a word-of-mouth-like cascade diffusion process wherein a message is actively forwarded from one person to other, within and between multiple weakly linked personal networks, resulting in a rapid increase in the number of people who are exposed to the message."[1] The three key attributes of virality, according to these authors, are (1) a person-to-person mode of diffusion; (2) great speed, which is enhanced by social media platforms; and (3) broad reach, which is achieved by bridging multiple networks. Hemsley and Mason, like other scholars researching virality, identify it as a certain diffusion process in which *a specific item* propagates in a certain way. This item is often tagged as a "viral video," "viral ad," or "viral photo."

The main difference between Internet memes and virals thus relates to variability: whereas the viral comprises *a single cultural unit* (such as a video, photo, or joke) that propagates in many copies, an Internet meme *is always a collection of texts*. You can identify a single video and say "This is a viral video" without referring to any other text, but this would not make much sense when describing an Internet meme. A single video is not an Internet meme but *part* of a meme— one manifestation of a group of texts that together can be described as the meme. Going back to "Leave Britney Alone," I would argue that Chris Crocker's video can be defined as a viral video that became a memetic video only with the emergence of its derivatives.[2] As elaborated in chapter 3, the "Leave Britney Alone" meme is composed of many videos. In a narrow, technical sense, both viral and memetic videos can be seen as adhering to Dawkins's idea of memes in that they spread gradually from person to person. However, memetic content is closer to the original idea of the meme as a living and changing entity that *is incorporated in the body and mind of its hosts*.

But this straightforward differentiation fails to capture the complex relationship between memes and virals. In pursuit of a more nuanced distinction, I put forward two assertions. First, we should think of the viral and the

Whereas the viral comprises a single cultural unit (such as a video, photo, or joke) that propagates in many copies, an Internet meme is always a collection of texts.

memetic as two ends of a dynamic spectrum rather than as a binary dichotomy. In fact, purely viral content probably does not exist—once a photo, or a video, reaches a certain degree of popularity on the Web, you can bet that someone, somewhere, will alter it. Moreover, there is a strong temporal element lurking here: many memetic videos started off as viral ones. Thus, if we think of the viral and the memetic as two ends of a dynamic spectrum, a more accurate differentiation would be threefold: (1) a *viral*: a single cultural unit (formulated in words, image or video) that is spread by multiple agents and is viewed by many millions. A "viral" may or may not have derivatives (see, for example, the Kony 2012 campaign, http:// invisiblechildren.com/kony/, or the Evian Roller Babies, http://youtu.be/XQcVllWpwGs); (2) a *founder-based meme*: an Internet meme that is sparked by a specific (often viral) text, video, or photo (such as "The Situation Room" or the "Pepper-Spraying Cop"). The "founding" unit is followed by many versions, each viewed by fewer people; and (3) an *egalitarian meme*: comprising many versions that seem to have evolved simultaneously without a clear founding text. As I will elaborate in chapter 7, egalitarian memes are often based on a certain formula or genre. Such memes are characterized by a more even popularity distribution between the various versions. Rage comics, LOLCats, and "*Hitler's Downfall* Parodies" would be examples of this category.

Table 1 Virals, founder-based, and egalitarian memes.

	Viral	Founder-based meme	Egalitarian meme
Number of versions	One*	Many	Many
Distribution of popularity	Millions of viewers of initial video	One (often viral) clip/photo that initiated the meme is by far the most popular	Popularity spreads quite evenly among numerous versions
Focus of derivatives		People relate to a specific photo or video	People relate to a certain formula
User involvement	Meta-comments	Modifying the text	Modifying the text
Examples	Evian Roller Babies	"Leave Britney Alone"	LOLCats

*When a viral generates many derivatives it can also be described as memetic.

My second assertion is that we should think of Internet memes and virals as different modes of engagement rather than as passive versus active formulations. Although it could be argued that viral diffusion is a more passive mode of communication than memetic imitation, I assert that both viral and memetic content involve engaged communication, albeit associated with different engagement levels. In the case of the viral, the communication may involve personalized meta-comments (for example, "Don't try this at home"), whereas memetic content invites modifications of the text itself.

While Internet memes and virals are similar in many respects, until now these concepts have been used in different ways in academic research. This split may stem from their association with two antithetic framings of communication—*communication as transmission* and *communication as ritual*. Articulated by James Carey in his book *Communication as Culture* (1989), this distinction provides fertile ground for mapping the new meme–viral scholarly landscape. The "transmission" standpoint likens the movement of goods or people in space to the spread of information through mass media. According to this view, communication is mainly a process of imparting information in the hope of augmenting the spread and effect of messages as they travel in space. To communicate effectively, on this view, is to "get your message through" to the masses quickly and without disturbances. By contrast, what Carey calls the "ritual" model defines communication not as the act of imparting information but as the construction and representation of shared beliefs. It highlights the sharedness of values, symbols, and cultural sensibilities that embody what people see as their communities. According to this view, the "message" in communication is not a unit whose reach and effect are easily traceable, but an ongoing process in which identities and senses of belonging are continually constructed.

Studies of virality tend to embrace the "transmission" model of communication. Virality-focused research—conducted mostly in the fields of marketing and political communication—focus on questions that relate to the diffusion of particular "items." They ask how and to what degree virals spread, investigate the factors that enhance their effectiveness, and chart the power structures underpinning this process. A prevalent question in politically oriented studies is what role do blogs and other social media play in the viral process—comparing it to the role played by established mass media outlets. For instance, in chapter 8 I will survey studies led by Kevin Wallsten and by Karine Nahon and her colleagues that focus on the diffusion of political clips in the 2008 US presidential campaign, and the role that official campaigners and bloggers had in augmenting the viral process.[3] In contrast, marketing-oriented studies—such as Phelps's and Berger and Milkman's analysis, discussed in chapter 6—tend to focus not on the processes or power structures underpinning viral diffusion but on successful strategies for viral marketing.

The handful of studies focusing on Internet memes (rather than virals) seems to be linked more strongly to Carey's second framing of communication as ritual. Such studies reflect the notion that memetic activities play an important role in constructing shared values in contemporary digital cultures. Treating memes as cultural building blocks, they attempt to understand people's memetic choices, as well as the meanings they ascribe to memes. The scholarship produced by Jean Burgess, Michele Knobel, Colin Lankshear, Patrick Davidson, and Ryan Milner—cited in various chapters of this book—reflects this fledging research trajectory.

An interesting way to move forward would be to invert the ways in which we study memes and virals, looking at viral content in terms of ritual, and examining memetic content in terms of transmission. In practice, this would require the evaluation of viral videos not only in terms of success or effectiveness but also in terms of their cultural implications and role in the formation of social and political identities. By contrast, an inspection of Internet memes from a transmission standpoint would focus on success factors and diffusion patterns. Such a "transmission"-oriented approach toward Internet memes is currently apparent mostly in the fields of information and computer science. Research there tends to focus on verbal memes, such as quotes, hash tags, or catchphrases, looking into the changes they undergo and the underlying factors that influence this process—such as utterance length and the source of the quote.[4]

In sum: while the borderline between "memes" and "virals" may be fuzzy, and in fact many videos and images are associated with both categories (by first spreading virally and then spawning numerous derivatives), it is still worth differentiating between them. In the next chapter, I will demonstrate that this distinction is especially useful when we think of the factors that motivate people to *share* content as opposed to those that augment users' tendency to *engage with it creatively*.

UNPACKING VIRAL AND MEMETIC SUCCESS

Now that we have a better grasp of what memes and virals are, it's time to delve into the sixty-four-million-dollar question: which features enhance the propagation of— and engagement with —Internet memes? The answer will unfold in two parts: first, I will tackle the issue of *virality*, that is, users' tendency to propagate certain types of content. Second, I will discuss the *memetic* qualities that enhance people's involvement with content by way of remaking, remixing, or imitating.

What Makes Content "Viral"?

Every day, each one of us is exposed to a mind-blowing amount of information: news and video clips; recipes and funny kittens; quizzes and weather alerts. Mostly, we pass. Sometimes, we read. And occasionally, we share: forward, post on our blog, tweet. While the decision to share or not to share is usually taken by individuals seated in isolation in front of their screens, research has revealed some of the patterns underlying these behaviors.

Jonah Berger and Katherine Milkman have conducted the most comprehensive study to date about the features that enhance sharing tendencies on the Internet. To explore what augments the "spreadability" of news items, the researchers examined a huge data set of nearly 7,000 *New York Times* articles published online, focusing on those that made it to the newspaper's list of most emailed stories.[1] Building on this work, as well as on more focused analyses of specific campaigns (particularly Kony 2012), I wish to highlight six factors that enhance content's virality. I label them as the "six Ps" (or the six-pack, for the marketers among you): *positivity*, *provocation of high-arousal emotions*, *participation*, *packaging*, *prestige*, and *positioning*.

(1) Positivity (and Humor)

One of Berger and Milkman's key findings is that people are more likely to share positive than negative stories. In addition, they prefer sharing items that are perceived as surprising, interesting, or practically useful. These preferences are explained as deriving from users' motivations of sharing content online. Since Internet users share for both social and self-presentation purposes, they prefer spreading content that makes others feel good and at the same time reflects on themselves as upbeat and entertaining. A news story about a rare elephant giving birth to twins in a tropical setting would probably cater well to both motivations: it puts a smile on the face of the person who gets it, and it will associate the sender with a positive, uplifting message.

This tendency toward positivity is in line with the growing body of evidence about the centrality of humorous content in viral processes. In their analysis of email forwarding, Joseph Phelps and his colleagues found that "jokes" was by far the largest forwarded content category. Similarly, Golan and Zaidner found that a striking majority (more than 90 percent) of advertisements produced by viral advertising companies include humorous elements.[2] In addition to the social and self-presentational benefits associated with positive content in general, humorous content may be particularly sharable as it tends to be surprising.[3] Surprise often invokes emotional arousal, which, as outlined below, is key for virality.

(2) Provoking "High-Arousal" Emotions

Berger and Milkman found that people share content that arouses them emotionally—both positively and negatively. Positive high-arousal is embedded in what the authors tag as "Awa" stories: pieces that generate a feeling of elevation in the face of something greater than oneself. Natural wonders, path-breaking scientific discoveries, and people overcoming adversities are prominent examples of narratives that generate "Awa" or "Wow" responses. "Awa" stories—combining positive valence and high levels of emotional arousal—were, by far, the most-forwarded stories in the *New York Times* list. But apparently, some less cheerful stories have become viral as well. These were stories that evoked negative high-arousal feelings of anger and anxiety. Such feelings activate people to do something—for example to share content. In contrast, stories that made people sad (but not angry or anxious) did not propagate very well—probably since sadness is a deactivating emotion.

The "Kony 2012" phenomenon illustrates vividly the relevance of high arousal for virality. Aired in March 2012 by the Invisible Children organization, this film launched a campaign to stop Joseph Kony's reign of terror, torture, and child abduction in Uganda. The film, which featured a young Ugandan whose brother was killed by Kony's army, as well as the director and founder of Invisible Children, Jason Russell, along with his young son, became an instant viral sensation. Within six days it reached 100 million viewers—spreading quicker than pop-culture-oriented hits such as Susan Boyle's appearance on *Britain's Got Talent* or Rebecca Black's "Friday." Part of the campaign's success relates to the fact that Kony 2012 made people angry: the crimes portrayed in the video were so outrageous, so shocking, and so extreme that remaining indifferent after watching it was almost impossible.

(3) Packaging

A pivotal aspect of viral diffusion is the packaging of messages. Berger and Milkman found that *clear and simple* news stories spread better than complex ones. Although unproven empirically, this principle may work for other genres and formats as well: simple videos or jokes could prove as more "sharable" since people understand them quickly and assume that others will decode them easily as well. Here, again, Kony 2012 provides a striking illustration. Simplicity is pivotal both in the videos' definition of the problem and in its proposed solution. An individual—Joseph Kony—is portrayed as the ultimate enemy, the worst villain on Earth. Since the problem is simple, the solution offered is equally straightforward. Users should double-click to influence policy makers and cover the streets with signs; America will then send soldiers to catch the bad guy and the world will be a better place. This straightforward and easy-to-digest message was regarded as important to the video's viral success; yet at the same time it was criticized as reducing a complex situation to simplistic frames.[4]

(4) Prestige

"Prestige" relates to users' knowledge about the content's source. With regard to news stories, it was found that the more famous the author is, the more likely people are to spread the piece. In other words: if you want to write a viral story, it will probably help if your name is Bill Gates or Brad Pitt. A similar tendency to rely on famous people—in a somewhat different configuration—is apparent in the diffusion of viral videos. Kony 2012's strategy, for instance, was to influence celebrities to support the cause publically by asking users to flood a defined list of celebrities and policy makers with premade tweets. This approach, tagged by Ethan Zuckerman as "attention philanthropy,"[5] generated public support of celebrities such as Oprah Winfrey, Rihanna, and Justin Bieber, further boosting the campaign.

(5) Positioning

According to Berger and Milkman, positioning is important for virality. In news stories, this manifests in the location of a certain article in digital space and time, based on editorial decisions. Unsurprisingly, stories featured for a long time in prominent locations on the *New York Times* home page tend to be more viral than those that are presented for shorter periods in less central locations.

Yet "positioning" may assume a broader meaning in the context of viral diffusion, which relates to the location of a message within social networks and to its association with certain actors. In viral marketing, the centrality of this feature is embedded in the emphasis on "seeding strategies," namely on the selection of the initial set of targeted consumers to whom the message is sent. Studies have shown that approaching the "right" users is crucial in the viral process. There are two types of preferred users for seeding: "hubs"—people with a high number of connections to others; and "bridges"—people who connect between otherwise unconnected parts of the network. Sending the initial message to these highly connected individuals has proved to be much more effective than sending it to "regular" users.[6]

In some cases, the forces that ignite the viral process are well-positioned and organized actors. According to Gilad Lotan's study, Kony 2012 was initially spread by a network of committed actors who had been supporters of the organization for a long time. These actors were clustered in several communities based in mid-sized cities such as Birmingham, Pittsburgh, and Oklahoma City. Many members of these seed networks identify themselves as young people with strong Christian faith. When the campaign was launched, they were ready for activation, and indeed contributed significantly to the ostensibly spontaneous viral spread of this message.[7]

The examples presented in this section demonstrate that positioning is influenced by both gatekeeping and strategic planning. Editors, advertisers, and activists can play a major role in processes that are seemingly free of formal control by positioning the article on the right website, or sending it to the right ultraconnected people.

(6) Participation

The five Ps presented so far seem to work well across many types of viral content. The last one, "participation," may be more relevant to viral-based political or commercial campaigns, in which sharing a particular piece of content is often a means to a different end such as boosting sales, winning an election, or changing a regime. What I mean by "participation" in this context is that viral dissemination may be enhanced if people are encouraged not only to share a certain item, but also to carry out other activities related to it.

Focusing on commercial campaigns, Odén and Larsson assert that viral success can be achieved when a campaign gives its audience an opportunity to engage and affect rather than just "pass through it."[8] In a similar vein, Ethan Zuckerman posits that a key component of Kony 2012's success was that it provided people with an opportunity to assert their influence via social media. Having seen the video and having been moved by it, users could actually do something with their rage, such as send a premade twitter message to a key policy maker. This additional activity deepened people's sense of involvement, vital for any political campaign.

Many successful campaigns depend not only on sharing content but also on the active engagement of users in re-creating or appropriating items. Lance Bennett and Alexandra Segerberg speak of such activities as "personalized content sharing" across media networks.[9] In chapter 8, I will focus on the example of the "We Are the 99 Percent" slogan of the Occupy Wall Street protest, showing how its appropriation into various contexts created a personal but universal narrative where, to cite Grant Meacham, "everybody is unique but in a similar situation."[10] Yet such modes of participation, as I will elaborate in chapter 8, are best understood not from a viral but from a memetic perspective.

What Makes Content Memetic?

Some virals are born and buried as virals. Others evolve to be memetic: content units that generate user-created derivatives in the form of remakes, parodies, or imitations. In this section, I look into the features of such memetic items, starting with video and moving on to photographs.

Memetic Videos

In a recent study, I asked: "Do YouTube videos that generate a high volume of derivatives share common features? And, if so, what are they?"[11] The first step in addressing this question was to identify "memetic videos"—exceptionally popular videos generating a high volume of derivative work. To do that, I used both YouTube's popularity measures of the top 100 "most viewed," "most responded," "most discussed," and "most favorited" videos, as well as user playlists of Internet memes. The list of candidate memetic videos was then screened by two coders to identify the videos that generated a substantial number of derivatives. These phases yielded a research corpus of thirty ultrapopular memetic videos.

At first glance, this group of memetic videos boasted such a dazzling array of seemingly unrelated features that finding any kind of common denominator appeared hopeless. After all, what could possibly connect a guy demonstrating weird dance maneuvers ("Evolution of Dance") with a face-painted boy declaring "I Like Turtles" ("Zombie Kid"); or an annoying dancing banana ("Peanut Butter Jelly Time") with a boy sticking his finger into his brother's mouth ("Charlie Bit My Finger")? Yet systematic qualitative and quantitative analysis did yield six common features amid this diversity: a focus on ordinary people, flawed masculinity, humor, simplicity, repetitiveness, and whimsical content.

1 Ordinary People The first feature of memetic videos reflects YouTube's famous focus on ordinary people. Seventeen texts in the sample feature ordinary folks whose fame can only be ascribed to their YouTube appearance, whereas only eight—all music videos—feature mass media celebrities. The "You-ness" of this group is also reflected in the sources producing the videos. Of thirty memes in the group, seventeen are clearly user-generated, ten were coded as originating in traditional media sources, and three could not be determined. While these numbers do not indicate a statistically significant advantage of ordinary-people-focused videos over celebrity-focused videos in the group, a comparison of our sample group with the pool of candidate memetic videos provides substantial evidence for this trend.

We reexamined the videos that were in our initial candidate meme pool but did not generate enough derivatives to be included in the sample group. The vast majority of these widely viewed videos (19 out of 22) were created by conventional media, mostly featuring celebrities. Comparing the videos that generated enough derivatives and were therefore included in the sample with those that did not meet our threshold indicated that popular user-generated videos tend to lure more derivatives than equivalent corporate or professional videos. These results suggest that if a user-created video achieves a certain level of popularity, it is more likely to generate a substantial number of derivatives than traditional content with the same number or even more viewings. In a similar vein, Jean Burgess and Joshua Green found that whereas traditionally generated videos are more common in YouTube's "most viewed" lists (66 percent), people tend to react more to user-generated videos. Such clips are more popular in the categories "most responded to" (video responses—63 percent) and "most discussed" (text-based responses—69 percent).[12]

But why do user-generated videos evoke more derivatives? One obvious answer is that this kind of production is simple, and thus easier to imitate (see below). Yet another key factor may be related to the videos' protagonists: ordinary people may set an achievable goal for others. Moreover, if we look at YouTube not just as a broadcasting platform but also as a community (following researchers such as Patricia Lange), then responding to a user-generated video seems to make more sense than responding to that of a celebrity, as we are communicating with peers. Our peers might even answer us or comment on our videoed responses, thus validating our imitation and our potential of attaining Internet fame. Yet, the protagonists of these videos are not just ordinary people; as we shall see, they tend to be ordinary men.

2   Flawed Masculinity   Although in the initial design of this study gender was not a prominent factor, a quick look at the sample required a change of plan. Men were the leading characters in twenty-four out of the thirty videos, while only three videos featured women as protagonists. This is not, however, simply a story about male hegemony, at least not in the conventional sense. Whereas in the three videos featuring women as leading characters ("Single Ladies," "Miss Teenage South Carolina," and "Paper Planes") the women adhere to conventional beauty standards prevalent in contemporary Western society, most of the men featured in these videos fail to meet prevalent expectations of masculinity either in appearance or behavior. Among the twenty-four videos, there are three overweight characters ("*Star Wars* Kid," "Numa Numa Guy," and the "Angry German Kid"); one little person ("Little Superstar"); one constantly perspiring individual with thick glasses ("Chocolate Rain"); and the fictional Leeroy Jenkins, who manages to get his entire group killed in a World of Warcraft game. Our collection includes videos featuring four young boys who also fail to represent the Western male model: "Zombie Kid"; baby Charlie and his big brother; and little David, shown under the effects of anesthesia ("David after Dentist"). Joining this cheerful bunch is Chris Crocker ("Leave Britney Alone"), an extrovertly expressive, effeminate homosexual.

The prominence of "flawed masculinity" in this collection of memetic videos can be seen as an extreme manifestation of men's representation in contemporary mass media genres, particularly the sitcom. Such genres have responded to the so-called crisis of masculinity in Western society by presenting far-from-perfect men who fail to fulfill basic functions in their personal and professional lives. Many sitcoms are characterized by ambivalent sexual politics: they embody a certain rebellion against hegemonic masculinity, yet at the same time reinforce traditional norms through the comic framing of their protagonists.

As in the case of sitcoms, flawed masculinity is presented in our corpus of memetic videos as comic and is thus associated with ambivalence. Unlike sitcoms, however, new meanings may be added to such videos through the discursive practices of the users who imitate them. A future exploration of the positions users take up when mimicking these videos—whether they mock or venerate their less-than-perfect masculine protagonists—is thus crucial for our understanding of the implications of this mode of representation.

3 Humor   Michele Knobel and Colin Lankshear found that humor served as a major component of successful memes created between 2000 and 2005.[13] In their analysis they assigned humorous texts to one of two categories: "quirky and situational humor," including dancing badgers, bizarre translations, and wacky teenagers; and "biting social commentary," in which humor was used to address a variety of political issues.

The present analysis of videos created mainly between 2006 and 2008 indicates that humor continues to be a key feature of Internet memes: no fewer than twenty-five of the thirty videos in the sample have a humorous aspect. But while quirky and situational humor is dominant in these videos, there was no trace of biting social commentary humor to be found in this specific group. This is not to say that politics does not find its way into Internet memes:

as I elaborate in chapter 8, it definitely does. Yet it is not a prominent feature of this group of extremely "memetic" videos. In ten clips, the protagonists are clearly trying to be funny; however, a larger group features individuals who do not (or at least do not obviously) intend to create humor. This category includes, for instance, films of animals and kids; protagonists who may or may not be acting out (e.g., "Angry German Kid," "Leave Britney Alone"); and colossal mistakes that people were unfortunate enough to be videoed making ("Miss Teenage South Carolina").

Three attributes of the comic seem to account for the prominence of humor in this sample of memetic videos: playfulness, incongruity, and superiority.

Playfulness   As described above, some videos in the group are clearly intended to be humorous. In these cases the comic tends to be intertwined with playfulness. In his seminal work *Homo ludens*, Johan Huizinga conceptualized play as an open-ended activity, in which people step out of real life "into a temporary sphere of activity with a disposition of its own." Like game-playing, humor is enjoyed for its own sake and involves a multilayered perception of social situations. Comic playfulness may thus lure user creativity by summoning viewers to take part in a game.

Incongruity   According to the incongruity theory of humor, comedy derives from an unexpected cognitive encounter between two incongruent elements, as in a pun, a man in women's clothing, or a dancing banana. Various forms of incongruity were found in the sample. For example, humans were juxtaposed with animals, and masculine traits with feminine ones. Among these incongruous structures, one emerged as particularly dominant: the fundamental yet often subtle incongruity between the audio and visual components of texts. In a few cases, such incongruity is embedded in the video format, most notably in lipsynch ("Numa Numa," for example); however, in others, it is derived from textual components unique to a specific video. For example, in "Chocolate Rain," incongruity stems from the contrast between the singer's boyish appearance and his low-pitched, mature male voice; in "Charlie Bit My Finger" we hear Charlie's big brother complaining about the biting, yet we see him deliberately sticking his finger into the baby's mouth.

Two features may explain the salience of audiovisual incongruity in our sample. First, this form of disharmony builds on the medium and its multimodality: the ability to convey both voice and image and to play with them through creative editing. But there may be more to it than that. In some cases, the gap between what we see and what we hear creates a dissonance, a puzzle that users may feel inclined to solve or further highlight by creating their own versions of the video.

Superiority   In some cases, play and incongruity are not what the video creators seem to have had in mind. Rather, they feature people who are unintentionally, or at least not clearly intentionally, funny. Here, a different attribute of humor—the association of the comic with superiority—may have a crucial role in generating remakes. Espoused in the writings of Plato and Aristotle and centuries later of Thomas Hobbes, superiority theory interprets laughter as an expression of the pleasant experience of one-upmanship. Superiority theories of humor may provide a simple explanation for the rocketing popularity of videos responding to memetic videos such as "David after Dentist," "*Star Wars* Kid," or "Miss Teenage South Carolina": some people enjoy not only watching videos of others whom they perceive to be inferior, but also take pleasure in scornfully imitating them, thus publicly demonstrating their own superiority.

4 Simplicity   Another prominent feature in this group of videos is simplicity. The vast majority of the videos were coded as employing a simple construction of their topics or ideas (that is, conveying one uncomplicated idea or slogan such as "It's peanut butter jelly time"). Simplicity is also a key feature of the videos' visual construction, as reflected in various attributes: most of the videos feature one or two performers, and even those with more participants usually focus on only one or two. In addition, half of the videos—for the most part user-generated—were not edited but rather were filmed in one take of a single shot. Another feature that emerged in the qualitative analysis is the simple design of the frames and settings in which the videos take place: some are shot against a plain white background (for example, "Leave Britney Alone"), others in a simple domestic setting ("Numa Numa"), or on a bare stage ("Evolution of Dance").

Simplicity is an important attribute contributing to the creation of user-generated versions of the meme. While any video can be edited or remixed, only a simple one can be imitated easily. It is almost impossible for an average user to create a persuasive emulation of the visual construction in Avril Lavigne's "Girlfriend" clip, yet one only needs a white piece of cloth, a camera, and a modicum of talent to remake "Leave Britney Alone." Simple videos enable people to emulate them in their own vernacular settings, with limited resources, and with low levels of digital literacy.

5 Repetitiveness Repetitiveness complements simplicity: most videos in the sample incorporate one simple unit that is repeated throughout the clip. Prominent examples include the highly repetitive lyrics and melody of "Chocolate Rain," a banana constantly jumping up and down in the "Peanut Butter Jelly Time" song, and Chris Crocker's recurring plea to "Leave Britney Alone." Simplicity and repetitiveness are found not only in user-generated content but also in several professional video clips in the sample, most notably Beyoncé's "Single Ladies." Filmed as a single sequence, the video features the singer and two Beyoncé look-alike dancers (that is, replicators) performing in front of a plain background and repeating the line "put a ring on it."

Repetitiveness may play an important role in encouraging active user involvement in remaking video memes. The meme itself includes a persuasive demonstration of its own replicability and therefore contains encrypted instructions for others' replications. In addition, repetitions enhance memorability, a feature described in the literature as important for memetic success.[14] Moreover, in some memetic videos, such as "Evolution of Dance" and "Numa Numa," repetition is intertwined with imitating a well-known person. Such videos are themselves imitations, calling for further imitation by others.

6 Whimsical Content The codebook for our study included a lengthy list of topics that were expected to appear in the videos; among them were sex, politics, the workplace, gender, race, ethnicity, sports, and religion. Coders were asked to mark the presence or absence of each topic in each of the videos. The analysis revealed that most anticipated topics did not appear in the corpus. Several did appear in a limited number of cases: traditional media content, such as pop music ("Evolution of Dance") and films ("*Star Wars* Kid") as well as the world of computers and gaming (Leeroy Jenkins and the "Angry German Kid"). If we combine these categories, it appears that the only content type somewhat salient in these memetic videos is related to popular culture. This referencing of pop culture may be connected to the videos' success. Since people may have different opinions on politics, religion, or sex, the moment any of these issues is injected, at least some people are bound to be alienated. But one can reasonably assume that most people contributing to YouTube know and appreciate popular culture, simply by dint of being on YouTube.

Aside from referencing pop culture, these memetic videos seem to share the absence of a concrete theme. Or, in other words, they demonstrate a tendency toward the whimsical (for example, "Zombie Kid" or "Charlie Bit My Finger"). In addition, they share a certain mode of presentation: depicting people playing or performing, often acting in a silly or irrational manner. This combination of playfulness and a lack of concrete content may in fact be regarded as an advantage when evaluating the tendency to replicate YouTube memes: users can imitate the playful spirit embedded in the texts, yet inject new themes according to personal preferences.

While not all memetic videos incorporate the whole set of six attributes, the most successful among them tend to integrate at least three or four. "Gangnam Style," for example, seems to encompass all six. Although PSY was popular in Korea, for the rest of the world he was completely anonymous until "Gangnam" went viral. Thus, the clip adheres to the "ordinary people" category. It also resonates well with the flawed masculinity attribute: PSY is something of a "weird bird" in the "K-pop" scene. Unlike most performers in the Korean pop music industry, he is not very young and does not adhere to conventional standards of beauty. The third memetic attribute—humor—is also evident in many aspects of this exaggerated and incongruous video. Simplicity seems to be the trickiest attribute to apply. At first glance, it does not fit this clip: "Gangnam Style" is a very rich text, adhering to professional production styles in its mise-en-scène and editing. Yet it incorporates some very simple and clear elements that stick out in the video's complex setting, particularly the words "Gangnam Style" and "sexy lady," and the unusual horse-riding dance performed by PSY. Moreover—and this leads me to the repetitiveness characteristic—most of these simple elements are repeated throughout the video time and again, demonstrating its own replicability. Finally, this video is as whimsical as it gets: it features a set of extremely quirky and bizarre situations coupled with lyrics that are utterly cryptic for anyone who does not know Korean. Interestingly, for Koreans this clip does have a concrete—and some say even satirical—framing, as it deals with identity practices of people who desperately try to look rich and successful, thus affiliating themselves with the luxurious neighborhood of Gangnam. But this meaning is evident only if you understand Korean; if you don't, the single message that seems to come through clearly is childish playfulness, which, as claimed above, seems to elicit more playfulness.

So far, I have presented each of the six memetic features separately and demonstrated how they all come to play in one ultramemetic video. Yet there is also a common thread among these features. Each of the six attributes found to be common to memetic videos—a focus on ordinary people, flawed masculinity, humor, simplicity, repetitiveness, and whimsical content—marks them as textually incomplete or flawed, and thus distinct from and perhaps defiant of glossy corporate content. Moreover, these memetic videos differ significantly from the viral videos that were included in our initial sample of highly viewed videos but did not generate enough derivatives to make it into the research group. Most of these excluded texts were visually rich, serious, and sophisticated music clips featuring celebrities.

This leads to a somewhat surprising conclusion: *"bad" texts make "good" memes in contemporary participatory culture.* Since the logic of contemporary participatory culture is based on the active involvement of users, incompleteness serves as a textual hook for further dialogue, and for

Thus, the ostensibly unfinished, unpolished, amateur-looking, and even weird video invites people to fill in the gaps, address the puzzles, or mock its creator.

the successful spread of the meme. Thus, the ostensibly unfinished, unpolished, amateur-looking, and even weird video invites people to fill in the gaps, address the puzzles, or mock its creator. This interpretation follows Henry Jenkins and his colleagues' description of gaps as enhancing the "spreadability" of content.[15] They depict incomplete and open-ended videos as epitomes of what John Fiske, writing about television, referred to as "producerly texts": media products in which gaps and inconsistencies invite viewers to "write in their absences," thus creating new meanings.[16]

A further conclusion relates to the fundamental complexity and elasticity of the meme concept. In this particular study, I conceptualized memes as texts—that is, videos with distinct visual layouts, participants, and plots. Yet, as I elaborated in chapter 4, the meme concept was originally thought of more expansively, incorporating social practices (such as celebrating birthdays) and ideas (such as belief in Heaven). And indeed, when exploring the corpus of videos studied here, bearing in mind the complex nature of memes, one can arrive at a higher-order understanding of memetic videos. It is the proposition that what is actually being replicated on YouTube is *the practice of creating simple and repetitive content*, which can be easily replicated and imitated by others. Thus, people are emulating not only specific videos, but the cluster of textual traits identified here as catalysts for imitation by others. Transplanting this to the realm of ideas would suggest that more than anything, *these memetic videos spread the notion of participatory culture itself*: a culture based on the active spread and re-creation of content by users.

Memetic Photos

So far, I have probed the question of what makes a video clip memetic. Now I shall address a similar query about memetic *photos*: photographs that attract extensive volumes of user-created responses, usually in the format of Photoshop-based collages. In order to systematically assemble such photos, I used the word "Photoshop" as a keyword in the huge database of "Know Your Meme" (http://knowyourmeme.com). I scanned all the results and analyzed only those that fit the category of memetic photos. Looking at this group of nearly fifty images, I asked: can we identify recurrent themes, forms, and stances of such photographs?

Well, yes we can. I divided the photos into two thematic groups: memetic photos featuring politicians and those devoted to other themes. I elaborate on political photos in chapter 8, and will focus my discussion here on the photos of ordinary people or entertainment celebrities. I suggest that these photos share two prevalent features: image juxtaposition and frozen motion.

Juxtaposition

A fundamental feature of many memetic photos is a striking incongruity between two or more elements in the frame. More specifically, what we often see is one person who sticks out as alien to the surrounding situation. The little "Frowning Flower Girl" at the royal wedding is the single grumpy face in a sea of grins, while the "Disaster Girl" smiles at the camera in front of a burning house.

These juxtapositions call for memetic responses: since the people featured in memetic photos appear to be out of context, their reappropriation to other contexts seems almost natural. Moreover, the sharp juxtapositions in the frame make some of the original memetic photographs look Photoshopped themselves, thus paving the way for similar Photoshop-based reactions. Users who capitalize on the incongruity embedded in the original memetic photo tend to do one of two things: to *deepen* the ridicule associated with the incongruity by presenting even stronger juxtapositions suggested by the original photo (for example, the "Disaster Girl" has not only set her house on fire, but she has also masterminded 9/11), or to *diminish* the initial incongruity by repositioning the character in a more appropriate context. For instance, in many versions the "Frowning Flower Girl" is relocated to situations that may be described as noisy disorder. When faced with circumstances such as the vuvuzelas during the World Cup or Rebecca Black's "Friday," putting your hands

Figure 7 Left: "Disaster Girl" and its memetic offspring. (Sources: http://jpgmag.com/photos/349763/ [photo courtesy of Dave Roth]; http://wierdwebsites.blogspot.co.il/.) Right: "Frowning Flower Girl" and its memetic offspring. (Sources: http://mashable.com/2011/04/30/frowning-flower-girl/; http://sonictruths.tumblr.com/post/5065937679/frowning-flower-girl-friday.)

over your ears to avoid unbearable noise seems perfectly logical.

In some cases, this incongruity between the actor and his or her surroundings assumes a grave moral guise. In such memetic photos, the protagonist either ignores or actively causes the suffering of others. Thus, the photo presenting Eden Abargil—a former Israeli soldier who posted photos of herself smiling beside bound and blindfolded Palestinian prisoners on Facebook—has much in common with the photo of Lieutenant John Pike, the "Pepper-Spraying Cop" described in chapter 4. Both photos present a contrast between a group of still, seated people and a single offender. In both, the wrongdoer seems to be utterly oblivious of the suffering he or she has caused. As discussed in chapter 4, memetic responses to such images may range from sardonic criticism to playful pastiche.

Frozen Motion

Another group of memetic photos depicts people in the midst of a physical activity such as running, dancing, or blowing soap bubbles. These photos feature both celebrities (such as Leonardo DiCaprio) and ordinary people (such as the "Bubble Girl"), who are captured during an intense movement that is "frozen in time" through photography.

Figure 8 "Still moving" images: "Bubble Girl" and "Leonardo DiHapprio." Sources: http://www.tumblr.com/tagged/chubby+bubbles+girl; http://forum .nin.com/bb/read.php?36,1144410,1144471.

A simple explanation for the extensive memetic reactions that such photos generate is that they tend to capture people in a somewhat ludicrous posture—in particular, it is the ungainly positioning of their bodies that makes people look funny. A further explanation would suggest that these photos capture a moment of great instability—people cannot remain in midair for more than a split second. Users are thus drawn to "join the action" and complete a seemingly unfinished movement.

Viral and Memetic Promoters: Commonalities and Differences

The main conclusion of this chapter is that viral and memetic promoters are not coextensive: the features that drive people to share content are not necessarily the same as those that draw them to imitate and remake it. Reevaluating the categories presented so far, I suggest a division into three groups of success factors, applicable to (a) both viral and memetic content, (b) viral content only, and (c) memetic content only.

Three features are related to both viral and memetic success: *simple packaging*, *humor* (and more generally, positive valence, when it relates to virals), and augmented *participation tools*. Simple packaging enhances content sharing: when people understand something quickly and

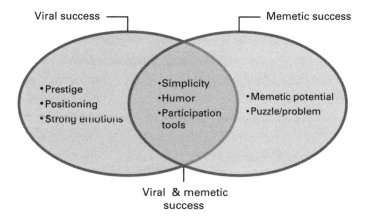

Figure 9 Viral and memetic success factors.

intuitively they are happy to forward it to others. It also encourages memetic responses, since simple content is easy to imitate. Humor augments sharing, as people wish to amuse their friends and to be associated with wittiness, but it also augments the tendency to imitate and remake content, given its association with playfulness, incongruity, and feelings of superiority. Finally, providing an assortment of participation tools (in addition to mere content diffusion) works well for viral campaigns, as people prefer to propagate content accompanied by "action points" that deepen their sense of agency and involvement. Yet such tools often lead to a transition from the "viral" to the "memetic," as users reappropriate and personalize universal content to describe their own cases.

Three criteria seem to be applicable particularly to viral (rather than memetic) success: *prestige*, *positioning*, and the *provocation of strong emotions*. In many ways, these features resonate with well-known success factors for mass-mediated items. A movie featuring flashy stars is more likely to succeed than one with an anonymous cast, a prime-time broadcast will draw more viewers than a show aired at dawn, and genres provoking strong emotions (such as thrillers) do particularly well at the box office. True, the motives for sharing content may differ from those driving people to watch it; when I send my friend a link to an infuriating movie about social injustice I also convey a message about my own moral standpoint. But putting motives aside and looking at the features themselves, the similarity between viral and mass-media success factors is striking.

The same is not the case for factors that enhance "memetic" creative responses. Based on my analysis so far, I can point to two factors that encourage memetic responses to both videos and photos: manifesting memetic potential and introducing a puzzle or problem. In videos, memetic potential is mainly demonstrated through *repetition*: repeating the same idea time and again improves the videos' prospects for successful replication. The memetic potential of many photographs is embedded in their Photoshop-like appearance. When the initial photograph already looks as if it had been Photoshopped, it elicits further Photoshopping and creative modifications. The second feature shared by memetic photos and videos is the appearance of a puzzle or problem that needs to be solved through creative responses. This puzzle often relates to the fundamental incongruities characterizing these texts, which again, seem to call out for the intervention of Internet users.

MEME GENRES

In theory, all Internet users are free spirits, individuals who take their unique path to the hall of digital fame. In practice, they tend to follow the same beaten tracks of meme creation. These paths can be thought of as *meme genres*. Defined as "socially recognized types of communicative action,"[1] genres share not only structures and stylistic features, but also themes, topics, and intended audiences. The study of genres encompasses both top-down cultural artifacts such as drama, film, and television, and bottom-up mundane types of rhetorical actions such as "best man" speeches and application letters. Recently, Internet meme genres have been added to the long list of genres that we encounter on a daily basis.

Internet meme genres are based on what Jean Burgess describes as "vernacular creativity":[2] everyday innovative and artistic practices that can be carried out by simple production means. Although vernacular creativity predates digital culture, Burgess suggests that new media have re-shaped it by turning hidden and mundane practices (such as singing in front of the mirror) into highly visible public culture. As public discourse, meme genres play an important role in the construction of group identity and social boundaries. Ryan Milner shows that while technically meme creation is becoming increasingly easy—specialized websites offer templates that even a six-year-old can operate—creating and understanding memes requires sophisticated "meme literacy."[3] In what follows, I assert that different meme genres involve different levels of literacy: some can be understood (and created) by almost anyone, whereas others require detailed knowledge about a digital meme subculture.

My selected list of nine meme genres is far from comprehensive, yet it surveys some of the central formats that have emerged in the past decade. It is written mainly as an introduction for those who are less immersed into digital culture. In other words: if you are a regular on 4chan, Tumblr, or Reddit, you may want to skip ahead to the next chapter.

Reaction Photoshops

Editing software in general and Adobe Photoshop in particular have been an inseparable part of Internet humor

Different meme genres involve different levels of literacy: some can be understood (and created) by almost anyone, whereas others require detailed knowledge about a digital meme subculture.

since the early 2000s.[4] The genre that I'm calling "reaction Photoshops" is composed of the images created in response to *memetic photos*, defined in chapter 6 as photographs that provoke extensive creative reactions. One of the earliest examples of a reaction Photoshop was the "Tourist Guy" meme. Shortly after 9/11, a photograph of a young man with sunglasses and a backpack standing on the World Trade Center observation deck, with a plane heading toward him, was widely circulated over the Internet. It soon became apparent that the photo was a hoax: a young Hungarian named Peter Guzli had edited a photo of himself—taken in 1997—and sent it to a couple of friends as a private joke. Once the hoax was exposed, the Internet was flooded by reaction Photoshops, showing the "tourist guy" in various settings and historical periods, spanning the sinking of the *Titanic*, the film *The Matrix*, and a Ku Klux Klan rally. Since reaction Photoshops are so prevalent, I discuss them at length in various parts of this book—particularly in chapters 6 and 8.

Photo Fads

The photo fad genre (as described by "Know Your Meme") includes staged photos of people who imitate specific positions or actions in various settings, usually with the purpose of posting the picture on the Web. Specific photo fad memes include, for instance, the ones described above as planking (lying face down with arms to the side in unusual settings) and "Heads in Freezers" (which is just what it sounds like), as well as "Put Shoe on Head" (ditto) and "owling" (sitting in a perched position and looking into the distance to imitate an owl). I provided a brief analysis of this genre in chapter 3. In many ways, it resembles the next genre on which I will elaborate.

Flash Mob

The flash mob is a phenomenon in which a group of strangers gather in a public space, suddenly and simultaneously perform a particular act, and after that just leave the scene, quick as a flash. The public act can assume many forms: frivolous dancing and freezing in place, zombie walks, and sudden disrobing. The gathering is coordinated through the Internet and mobile phones, and then photographed and uploaded to YouTube.

Flash mobs emerged as an Internet phenomenon in 2003, when over one hundred people flooded the home furnishings department of Macy's in Manhattan. They told the sales assistants they were members of a commune living in a warehouse in Williamsburg and were looking to buy a "love rug" for the price of $10,000 "to play on." Bill Wasik, then a senior editor of *Harper's Magazine*, was credited with organizing this prank and consequently with the invention of the flash mob genre, which quickly spread outside New York City and the United States.

Virág Molnár traces the roots of the genre to twentieth-century avant-garde movements, such as the Dadaists, who wanted to shock the conformist "bourgeois" middle classes by using surprise and guerilla tactics.[5] For instance, the US-based Yippies (members of the Youth International Party), an amalgam of apolitical hippies and radical New Left activists, engaged in politically oriented pranks. In one of them, a group of Yippies took a tour of the New York Stock Exchange and started throwing dollar bills onto the trading floor. Trade was stopped as elegantly dressed brokers stumbled over each other to get to the money.

According to Molnár's typology, contemporary flash mobs include several subtypes. While some of these are apolitical, others have an embedded anticonsumerist element: they want to "reclaim" public space that has been overtaken by commercial use and interests in order to generate consumption-free enjoyment. Yet, somewhat ironically, from an early stage the genre was capitalized on for marketing purposes. For instance, the cellular company T-Mobile coordinated a flash mob dance of three hundred people at a London train station, resulting in an extremely popular YouTube advertisement. This commercial use has been criticized as subverting the basic principles of the genre: democracy, anticommercialism, and spontaneity.

Lipsynch

Lipsynch (or lipdub) videos are clips in which an individual or group is seen matching their lip movements to a popular song. Before the 1970s, lipsynch was used widely as a technical—yet concealed—procedure in popular music performance and cinema: the audience was not supposed to see any disconnection between voice and body. Even now, exposure of lipsynching elicits mockery and accusations of lack of authenticity. The origins of lipdub as a performative genre, in which the split between voice and body is manifest and played upon, can be traced to Dennis Potter's TV series *Pennies from Heaven* (1978). The series featured a 1930s salesman who avoided the agonies of his life by escaping, through lipsynch, to the magical world of music. In Potter's later productions—*The Singing Detective*, *Lipstick on Your Collar*, and *Karaoke*—lipsynching was further developed as a technique through which the ideas and emotions of the characters were exposed.[6]

The Internet, and especially the introduction of personal webcams and, later on, simple editing software, has enabled the quick popularization of the genre. Indeed, lipsynching has become extremely prevalent across the globe. It currently embeds two main subgenres: bedroom lipdubs and collective lipdubs. As I outline below, the first subgenre is linked to private households and the second to public activities and organizations.

Bedroom lipsynchs feature a small number of participants, usually in front of their webcams. One of the first notable examples of this genre was the "Numa Numa" dance, performed by Gari Brolsma in 2004. Brolsma, a nineteen-year-old student from New Jersey, just wanted to entertain his friends with a personal version of the Romanian hit "Dragostea Din Tei." But apparently the video amused other people as well: within a short period, it had been viewed by millions, evoking numerous memetic responses, in the form of both flattering homage and derogatory mockery. Another notable example is the "Back-Dorm Boys," two Chinese art students from Guangdong Province who, in 2005, uploaded a lipsynched version of the Backstreet Boys hit "I Want It That Way." Their overwhelming popularity resulted in a subsequent series of videos and vast mainstream media attention. Such success stories encouraged many others, resulting in numerous bedroom lipsynchs covering almost every imaginable pop hit. The memetic appeal of this genre can be explained in light of the principles discussed in chapter 3. Bedroom lipdubs are very easy to produce, and they relate strongly to today's era of networked individualism. They highlight the presence and talents of a specific individual, and also signal that this person is part of a larger digital pop culture.

In contrast to the individualistic aura of bedroom lipsynchs, public sphere lipsynchs are multiparticipant collective productions. They are often created as an organizational effort, featured in spaces such as university campuses, offices, or army bases, and filmed in one continuous camera shot. This subgenre has also been labeled lipdub, a term coined in 2006 by Jakob Lodwick, the founder of Vimeo (a video-sharing venture that allows only user-generated material). Lodwick explains: "It's kind of the bridge between amateur video and actual music videos."[7] Collective lipdubs are often used for public relations. They signify to the world that a certain university or firm is "cool," vigorous, and frivolous—the kind of place you would like to be.

Both types of lipdub embody a blend of fame and anonymity that characterize participatory culture. Lipdubs are based on the reappropriation of mass-mediated hits, originally performed by professional singers, by small, local communities of amateurs. While this may be seen as a positive, democratizing turn, a more critical reading claims that lipdub also draws a line between amateur and professional art: most lipsynchers remain anonymous, and even if they do become famous, they are labeled as class B YouTube stars who are never equivalent to "real" film or television stars. Moreover, as Graham Turner suggests, success in digital media is still measured through one's ability to be incorporated into traditional mass media.[8] Thus, genres such as lipsynch do not create a real alternative to the conventional media industries.

Misheard Lyrics

Phonetic translation or misheard-lyrics videos are based on amusing mistranslations of spoken sounds to written words. These are done by transcribing what the words sound like (that is, their phonetics), regardless of their true meaning. Phonetic translations were molded into a distinct meme genre following a popular 2001 animation that Neil Cicierega created to the Japanese song "Hyaku-gojyuuichi." At a certain point, subtitles such as "Give my sweater back or I will play the guitar" popped on the screen, reflecting what the Japanese words would sound like to an average English speaker. In subsequent years, many similar clips (tagged as "animutations") emerged on the Internet.[9]

At a later stage, another phonetic translation subgenre emerged based on an even simpler user-generated manipulation: the insertion of subtitles into an existing video clip, usually one that originated in South or East Asia. This subversion is sometimes called "buffalax," referring to the nickname of the YouTuber who in 2007 posted the staple video of this subgenre, "Benny Lava." His phonetic translation of the song "Kalluri Vaanil" by Tamil artists Prabhu Deva and Jaya Sheel opens with the unforgettable line: "My loony bun is fine, Benny Lava!," followed by such gems as "Have you been high today? I see the nuns are gay." The genre quickly globalized, with numerous linguistic dyads emerging, including, for example, Malayalam subtitles to a Russian folksong. English language songs, heard (but not always understood) the world over, have also became popular targets. For instance the Beatles' "I Want to Hold Your Hand" is phonetically translated into Japanese as "Stupid public urination," and "I've Got the Power" becomes in German "Agathe Bauer."[10]

Recut Trailers

A recut trailer is a user-generated "fake" movie trailer based on the re-editing or remixing of film footage. In many cases, it displaces the original film's genre with an utterly different one, creating "new" movies such as *Brokeback to the Future* (an amalgam between *Brokeback Mountain* and *Back to the Future*) and *Scary Mary Poppins*. The genre was popularized in 2005, with the launch of the trailer for *The Shining*, which presented the famous horror film as a delightful family comedy featuring a story of father–son bonding.

Kathleen Williams unpacks some of the paradoxes underpinning recut trailers. While their very existence clearly indicates that people are familiar with (and even enjoy) movie trailers, these clips are also saturated with criticism of the trailers' blunt marketing strategies. Specifically, recut trailers mock the formula-based and mechanistic ways in which marketers try to press audience's emotional buttons. For instance, a recut trailer that presents the horror film *Jaws* as a romantic comedy uses the narration, "In a world that does not understand ... in a place where there is no hope at all ... love comes to the surface." The incongruity between these motivational words and what we know about the film parodies the original trailers' overly optimistic scripts of overcoming adversaries. Moreover, recut trailers reflect the ambivalent nature of audiences' relationship with pop culture in the Web 2.0 era.[11] While professional trailers are released and consumed according to industry-dictated timing, recut trailers reflect the new power claimed by Internet users who play with cinema without actually needing "to go to cinema at all."[12] Yet although these parodied trailers seemingly promote nothing, they actually do promote something: the image of their creators as talented, creative, and digitally literate people.

LOLCats

LOLCats are pictures of cats accompanied by systematically misspelled captions, which typically refer to the situation shown in the photo. The genre's name is a composite of the Internet acronym "LOL" (laughing out loud) and the word "cat." It was the first prominent manifestation of "image macros": a more general form of pictures with overlaid text. The spike in this genre's popularity is associated with the image-posting board I Can Has Cheezburger? (http://icanhas.cheezburger.com), launched in 2007. Motivated by the urge to understand "Why in the name of Ceiling Cat are LOLCats so popular," Kate Miltner investigated the appeal of the genre by interviewing LOLCat lovers.[13] She found that the LOLCat audience actually comprises three separate groups: CheezFrenz (who like LOLCats because they love cats), MemeGeeks (who love LOLCats because they acknowledge the genre's place in the grand history of Internet memes), and casual users (all the rest, mostly composed of the "bored at work" population).

Miltner found that beyond these differences, LOL-Cats are used to construct and maintain social boundaries. Creating—and enjoying—LOLCats requires familiarity with the genre and the special language underpinning it, "LOLspeak." This is a complex, nonstandard, childlike (or catlike) English Internet dialect, which is celebrated by its users as "teh furst language born of teh intertubes." Enjoying the genre involves the sweet scent of an inside joke, understood by those who are immersed in the digital cultural landscape. In addition, in many cases LOLCats are created or shared for the purpose of interpersonal communication: they serve as indirect ways to convey a wide array of feelings and states of mind. Thus, although LOLCats are often dismissed as emblems of a silly and whimsical culture, Miltner shows that they actually fulfill diverse and complex social roles.

Stock Character Macros

The stock character macros meme genre originated from one meme, labeled "Advice Dog." The initial meme, featuring a photo of a puppy's face positioned on a multicolored rainbow background, was launched on a 2006 discussion board on which a boy asked for romantic advice about kissing a girl. The photo of the dog advising "Just do it" spurred a stream of derivatives on 4chan, featuring the dog offering further pieces of bad advice. This then prompted a profusion of related "advice animal" memes, such as "Socially Awkward Penguin," the aggressive "Courage Wolf," and "Bachelor Frog."[14]

While the genre is commonly labeled "advice animals," it does not always include advice, and, over time, many human protagonists have been added to the initial animal-based arsenal. Yet memes belonging to this family do share two features: they use image macros, and they build on a set of stock characters that represent stereotypical behaviors. A very partial list of macro characters includes "Scumbag Steve" (who always acts in unethical, irresponsible, and asocial ways) and his antithesis, "Good Guy Greg" (who always tries to help, even if it brings him harm); "Naive College Freshman" (who is overenthusiastic about his new status as a student and clueless about the norms of social behavior in college); "Annoying Facebook Girl" (who is overenthusiastic and overanxious about Facebook and its significance to her social life); "Female College Liberal" (also known as "Bad Argument Hippie," who is both naive and a hypocrite); "Success Kid" (a baby with a self-satisfied grin, accompanied by a caption describing a situation that works better than expected); and "Successful Black Man" (a black man who comically subverts racist assumptions about him by acting like a middle class bourgeois). This array of stock character macros provides a glimpse into the drama of morality of the First World of the twenty-first century: it is a conceptual map of types that represent exaggerated forms of behavior. As detailed below, these extreme forms tend to focus on success and failure in the social life of a particular group.

Rage Comics

Rage comics are amateur-looking comics featuring "rage faces"—a set of expressive characters, each associated with a typical behavior. The genre embarked on 4chan in 2008 with a stream of four-panel comics dedicated to the tales of a character named the Rage Guy, who was often caught in situations that led him to scream in anger

(FFFFFFUUUUUUUU). Following the success of this initial rage face, a series of neighboring characters shortly emerged, among them Forever Alone (a sad, lonely chap with no friends); Me Gusta ("I like" in Spanish, a character who expresses enjoyment); Troll Face (who enjoys annoying and harming people); and Poker Face (who tries to conceal his embarrassment in awkward situations). Since then, rage comics have migrated from 4chan into other communities, expanding the range of faces in the repertoire. The means for creating rage comics were also popularized, with the introduction of "Rage Makers" websites, on which users can create rage comics easily by reappropriating readymade characters. Yet, as Ryan Milner observes, digital literacy is not enough in order to participate in the rage discourse. It also requires subcultural literacy: knowledge of the codes and norms developed in this meme-based subculture. Thus, one needs to have a considerable amount of knowledge about a large number of characters and the socially appropriate ways to use them in order to create an ostensibly simple four-panel comic.

Although rage comics and image macros differ in format, they deal with similar themes. According to Ryan Milner's illuminating analysis, these meme genres tend to focus on a small core of subjects associated with winners

Figure 10   Stock character macros: "Scumbag Steve," "Success Kid," and "Socially Awkward Penguin." Source: http://www.quickmeme.com/.

Figure 11 Rage comics. Source: http://fuckyeahchallengeacceptedguy .tumblr.com/.

and losers in social life. He tags them as "Fail," "What the fuck," and "Win" memes. "Fail" marks moments of social incompetence, embarrassment, and misfortune and is incarnated in specific characters (such as "Forever Alone" and "Socially Awkward Penguin"), as well as in the narrative structure of many rage comics that end with a moment of personal failure. In numerous cases, failure has to do with geeky or awkward young men's lack of romantic success, often associated with Net subcultures. Posters often accompany these memes with commentary such as "This happened to me today," thus using the memes as a "way to share geeky failure in a collective way."[15] "What the fuck" (or WTF) memes relate to those instances in which failure is not associated with the self, but with others, leaving the protagonist with the eternal question, WTF? The "others" in such memes are framed as the out-group. They lack intelligence, discernment, and literacy—particularly digital literacy. Finally, "Win" memes deal with successful social interactions and small daily victories that help the protagonist avoid "a Forever Alone fate."[16]

In this chapter, I have presented nine major Internet meme genres, as a first step in mapping a complex universe of user-generated content. As evident from this survey, some of these genres have already been studied in depth, while others have attracted less scholarly attention. Yet to obtain a fuller understanding of the memesphere, an integrative and comparative analysis of these genres is required. An initial observation stemming from this survey is that meme genres can be divided into three groups: (1) Genres that are based on the *documentation of "real-life" moments* (photo fads, flash mobs). These genres are always anchored in a concrete and nondigital space. (2) Genres that are based on *explicit manipulation* of visual or audiovisual mass-mediated content (reaction Photoshops, lipdubs, misheard lyrics, recut trailers). These genres—which may be grouped as "remix" memes—often reappropriate news and popular culture items. Such transformative works reveal multifaceted attitudes of enchantment and criticism toward contemporary pop-culture. (3) Genres that evolved around *a new universe of digital and meme-oriented content* (LOLCats, rage comics, and stock character macros). These genres, emerging mainly after 2007, embody the development of a complex grid of signs that only those "in the know" can decipher. Thus, in order to produce and understand LOLCats, users need to master LOLspeak; to create a rage comic, the user requires familiarity with a broad range of new symbols. These genres are thus strongly associated with what Ryan Milner describes as the meme subculture, which flourishes on specific sites such as 4chan, Tumblr, and Reddit. Yet since all nine genres that I have surveyed in this chapter are still alive and kicking, users who are not part of this subculture still have a wide spectrum of options for creating and consuming Internet memes.

MAY THE EXCESSIVE FORCE BE WITH YOU: MEMES AS POLITICAL PARTICIPATION

The Web was invented so physicists could share research papers. Web 2.0 was invented so we could share cute pictures of our cats. The tools of Web 2.0, while designed for mundane uses, can be extremely powerful in the hands of digital activists, especially those in environments where free speech is limited.

—Ethan Zuckerman, "The Cute Cat Theory of Digital Activism"

This chapter focuses on a new amalgamation of cute cats and hard-core politics: *political memes*. Politics—both in its broad sense as the societal construction of power and in its narrow sense as a system of governance—is deeply intertwined with the construction and consumption of Internet memes. In the following pages, I will explore memes as forms of political participation, looking into both democratic and nondemocratic settings. This inspection will elucidate the distinction between Internet memes and

Internet humor: while some political memes are framed in a humorous manner, others are deadly serious. But regardless of their emotional keying, political memes are about making a point—participating in a normative debate about how the world should look and the best way to get there.

The general prism through which I explore political memes is that of *political participation*. Whereas traditional political-science accounts of participation have focused on easily measurable practices, such as voting or joining political organizations, in recent years the perception of what constitutes political participation has been broadened to include mundane practices, such as commenting on political blogs and posting jokes about politicians. To a large extent, this transformed perception of what counts as political participation is tied to the rise of the Internet and other digital media. New media offer appealing and convenient ways to stimulate participatory activity, especially among younger citizens who have been the least likely to participate in formal politics.[1]

The centrality of new media in contemporary politics was strongly demonstrated in the 2008 US presidential election campaign. Heralded as the first Web 2.0 campaign, these elections were characterized by massive amounts of politically oriented user-generated content. Social media like YouTube and Facebook played an important role in these elections and were exploited by all candidates, but

But regardless of their emotional keying, political memes are about making a point—participating in a normative debate about how the world should look and the best way to get there.

especially by Barack Obama. The innovative use of digital media in his campaign mobilized supporters into action in multifaceted and unprecedented ways.

New media proved to be pivotal not only in top-down political campaigns, but also in grassroots social and political movements. In 2011, *Time* magazine crowned "The Protester" as its "Person of the Year," referring to the massive and effective street protests seen around the globe in that period. It began with the so-called Arab Spring—when protesters joined forces in Tunisia, Egypt, and other countries to put an end to corrupt dictatorships. Soon the idea of mass protests became memetic: in New York and Moscow, Madrid and Tel-Aviv, millions of people occupied the streets protesting injustices and flawed policies. Though the motivations for these protests were varied and the stakes different, in all cases the protesters made extensive use of new media for organization, persuasion, and mobilization.[2]

Memes and virals have played an important role within this new landscape of Web-based political participation, both in grassroots and top-down campaigns. In this chapter, I suggest that Internet-based political memes fulfill three interwoven functions:

(1) *Memes as forms of persuasion or political advocacy.* The extensive use of memes in recent election campaigns has

demonstrated their persuasive capability. As I outline below, the majority of studies on this issue have looked into virals (rather than memes), attempting to gauge their influence and diffusion patterns.

(2) *Memes as grassroots action.* Building on Lance Bennett and Alexandra Segerberg's notion of digital "connective action,"[3] I will discuss the central role of memes in linking the personal and the political to empower coordinated action by citizens.

(3) *Memes as modes of expression and public discussion.* Meme creation is an accessible, cheap, and enjoyable route for voicing one's political opinions. As a result, any major event of the past few years has generated a flux of commentary memes. Drawing on Ryan Milner's notion that memes constitute spaces of polyvocal expression in which multiple opinions and identities are negotiated,[4] I will look into recent examples of these meme-driven discourses.

These three functions of political memes are manifest in both democratic and nondemocratic contexts. Yet, as I will elaborate in the last section of this chapter, in nondemocratic environments Internet memes may bear an additional important meaning of *democratic subversion*.

Memes (and Virals) as Persuasion: The 2008 US Presidential Campaign

Within the vibrant universe of online activities during the 2008 campaign, watching and spreading audiovisual content was particularly common. Clips such as "Obama Girl," "Wassup," and "Yes We Can" attracted millions of viewers and commanded considerable public and scholarly attention. This interest in political virals derives from the assumption that such videos may be highly influential. As early as the 1950s, Elihu Katz and Paul Lazarsfeld showed that people listen to what their neighbors, family, and community members have to say about politics.[5] They found that personal influence is a pivotal aspect of persuasion—probably more important than mass-media messages. It is not surprising, then, that people are expected to treat political ads forwarded to them by their friends and colleagues more favorably than standard broadcasted ones. Moreover, virality itself is considered to be highly persuasive: raw "view-count" numbers inform viewers that many others have found a particular piece of content interesting.

While it is agreed that viral videos may bear considerable political impact, many questions remain about their sources, content, and diffusion patterns. Based on a vast number of political videos from the 2008 campaign, Travis Ridout and colleagues examined whether YouTube enables new voices and forms of expression to enter the political process.[6] In theory, any person can create a political viral. But does it actually happen? An analysis of 3,880 election-driven YouTube clips that passed the threshold of 1,000 views yielded interesting results. On one hand, the researchers found that the vast majority of such clips were posted by traditional actors, mostly the official campaigns. However, when they broke down the data to the number of views per clip, they found a strong bias toward nontraditional political actors. Thus, whereas typical party-sponsored ads had an average of 55,000 views and typical candidate-sponsored ads had just over 60,000, interest-group-sponsored ads yielded 139,000 views, citizen-designed ads averaged 807,000 views, and ads created by other entities (mostly media companies, small news organizations, groups of bloggers, or small video production groups) averaged a startling 2.5 million-plus views. This finding is corroborated by an examination of the most viral videos—only a fifth of them were produced by the campaigners, and in all cases they were not typical ads, but edited footage (such as Obama dancing on *The Ellen DeGeneres Show*). Yet, it is important to note that these viral videos were not produced "by a lone citizen, armed with only a camera and a cause." Interest groups and other nontraditional actors who produced the 2008 virals were established organizations backed by financial and social resources.

Clips created by such well-resourced groups often bear the esthetics of professional media content. For instance, "Yes We Can"—widely acknowledged as the most influential music video during the campaign—was produced by a group of Obama-supporting artists. It combines images from two sources—television footage of Obama's speech after the New Hampshire primary and celebrity appearances by stars like Scarlett Johansson, Kate Walsh, and Kareem Abdul-Jabbar. Though the clip is shot in a simple setting of a black background, it is neatly crafted by professionals like hip hop artist Will.i.am, director Jesse Dylan, and cinematographer Rolf Kestermann.

The success of this video led Kevin Wallsten to explore the factors and actors that enhanced its spreadability.[7] He found that members of the Obama campaign played an important role in this process. Campaign member statements significantly influenced not only the number of views, but the amount of discussion about it in the blogosphere, as well as the clip's coverage in the media. Although the video itself was not produced as part of the official campaign, being embraced by it was crucial to its going viral. Another pivotal actor in the diffusion of the clip was bloggers: discussion of the clip in blogs drew the attention of both Internet users and journalists. Wallsten's study thus corroborated the central role of political blogs in the diffusion of political content. While this may sound like an optimistic finding, further large-scale analysis of the types of blogs that influence virality suggests a clear hierarchy within the blogoshere. Karine Nahon and her colleagues analyzed data on nearly 10,000 blogs and 13,000 blog posts linking to 65 of the top viral videos in the presidential election.[8] The authors show that a small group of blogs—which they tag "elite blogs" and "top-general" blogs—ignite the viral process. Once these blogs link to a video and "crown" it as viral, other blogs—such as political blogs and "tail" blogs, tend to follow. Their study thus demonstrates that a small group of powerful actors has a large influence on the process of viral diffusion.

Memes as Political Action and Discourse: Occupy Wall Street and Memetic Photos

Whereas existing analysis of viral videos in the context of persuasion and political campaigns tends to highlight the ways power comes into play in an allegedly egalitarian sphere, the analysis of memes as political action tends to stress their role in *citizen empowerment.* Looking into activist movements in the past decade, Lance Bennett and Alexandra Segerberg[9] identify two types of logic (or structural principles) that govern contemporary digital political action. The first is the well-known "old" logic of collective action, associated with high levels of organizational resources and the formation of group identities. The Internet has made it easier to engage in collective action, but has not changed it in a fundamental sense. Thus, for instance, an NGO like Greenpeace has benefited greatly from new media, but is still dependent on its loyal group of supporters and its "offline" resources. Yet recently, another structure of political action has become prevalent worldwide. This second logic, labeled "connective action," is based on personalized content sharing across media networks. Connective action emerged in an era in which formal organizations' influence over individuals is declining and strong ties between people and the groups to which they belong are being replaced by large-scale, fluid social networks. As more and more people share their opinions and criticisms with networked peers, technology platforms begin to take the place of established organizations. Protests such as the Spanish Los Indignados (the Indignant Ones) or the American Occupy Wall Street are not backed by a strong existing organization—they are energized by the digitally coordinated actions of millions of ordinary people.

Memes play an important role in these coordinated actions. Shared slogans that travel easily across large and diverse populations are essential to stimulating thousands or millions of people to take up a cause. Yet the power of these campaigns, according to Bennett and Segerberg, stems from the fact that their general messages or slogans do not prorogate in a single mode: they are personalized, adapted by individuals to tell their own stories. Thus, for instance, the central website for "Put People First"—a civil society platform calling for an economy based on environmental considerations and fair distribution of wealth—presented an empty text box under an image of a megaphone, inviting the visitor to "Send Your Own Message to the G20." In response, users applied the catchy slogan "Put People First," connecting it to their personal backgrounds. A similar process took place around the "We Are the 99 Percent" meme, which I shall address shortly.

The perception emerging from Bennett and Segerberg's analysis is that *memes serve as pivotal links between the personal and the political*. Since they are based on shared frameworks that call for variation, memes allow citizens to participate in public, collective actions, while maintaining their sense of individuality. The role that memes play in connective action is thus the political manifestation of what I described in chapter 3 as the compatibility between memes and "networked individualism." Yet the personalization of political memes is beneficial not only to the individuals spreading them. As I will demonstrate through the case of the "99 Percent," personalized memes also serve the rhetoric of political movements.

Occupy Wall Street, 2011

The prevalent role played by memes in grassroots "connective action" was strongly manifest in Occupy Wall Street—a protest movement criticizing social and economic injustices in the United States. The strong connection be-tween this movement and memetic activity is rooted in the identity of its initiators—the editors of the Canadian magazine *Adbusters*. One of them, Kalle Lasn, suggested in a manifesto titled *Culture Jam: The Uncooling of America* that readers should resist the corporate messages that dominate American media through creative vandalism and mock-advertisements. Lasn was one of the first activ-ists to use memes as an integral part of his rhetoric, claim-ing that in order to resist the memes produced by large corporations, people should create and circulate subver-sive "countermemes." For instance, in a satire on a Tommy Hilfiger ad, the brand's name was rewritten to read "To My Ill Figure," highlighting the role of major fashion brands in promoting unrealistically thin body images. This practice of altering consumer icons in ways that charge them with new subversive meanings has been labeled "culture jam-ming." While the term was coined in the early 1990s, it emerged as a mass practice only in the twenty-first cen-tury, stimulated by the blend of user-friendly image-edit-ing software and the ubiquitous presence of social media through which millions can jam.

Given the identity of Occupy's founders, it is not sur-prising that the very conception of the movement in Sep-tember 2011 was intertwined with memetic activity. The initial email sent out by *Adbusters* to its mailing list about the forthcoming protests was accompanied by a poster of a

Figure 12   Culture jamming. Source: http://subvertise-antidot.blogspot
.co.il/2009_01_01_archive.html.

graceful ballerina pirouetting on top of Wall Street's iconic charging bull statue.[10] It adhered to the familiar *Adbusters* aesthetic of taking a famous corporate icon and subversively repositioning it, thus calling for further interrogation and criticism of taken-for-granted symbols.

And indeed, the ballerina on the charging bull was the first in a surge of memes that accompanied the protests. Ryan Milner, who provides an extensive analysis of the Occupy memes, asserts that such forms of amateur participation made a perfect fit with the movement's egalitarian and nonauthoritative ethos. To a large extent, the protests were energized and backed by the Web's prominent meme hubs, particularly Reddit and Tumblr. However, the memetic activity surrounding Occupy was not one-sided. As the protests evolved, a rich variety of opinions were exposed through the posting of memes and countermemes. While numerous voices supported the protests, many others were opposed to it. This rich, multifaceted discussion is framed by Milner as a polyvocal quality of meme-based discourse, through which diverse opinions and identities are expressed and negotiated. He demonstrates this quality through a detailed analysis of the flagship meme of the protest, "We Are the 99 Percent."

This slogan relates to the argument that 1 percent of the American population controls almost all the country's

Figure 13   The memetic initiation of Occupy Wall Street. Source: http://noclexington.com/?p=5363.

WHAT
IS OUR
ONE
DEMAND?
#OCCUPYWALLSTREET
SEPTEMBER 17TH.
BRING TENT.

financial wealth. Early on in the campaign, it was molded into a meme with a particular aesthetics: a person holds a handwritten text depicting her or his gloomy story, leading to the shared motto "I am the 99 percent." This meme's power stems from the way in which its three memetic dimensions of form, content, and stance re-enforce each other. Its message about the agonies of ordinary Americans is conveyed by average-looking people with serious facial expressions holding similar amateurish-looking signs. This combination of repetition and variation turns the personal to political: Stories about the sick young woman who is unable to afford medication, the single mom who struggles to provide for her son, and the father who cannot send his daughter to college are reframed as particular cases of the same flawed structure. These people's miseries are not just personal problems; they stem from the systemic economic and political illnesses of their habitat.

The popularity of the "99 percent" meme soon generated a countermeme, in which the aesthetics and rhetoric of the original meme were played against it: the "53 percent" meme. Created by conservative activists, it referred to the premise that only 53 percent of American people pay income tax. In this countermeme, personal stories of hard-working people who pay taxes and refrain from complaints portray Occupy protesters as the 47 percent of the

Figure 14   "We Are the 99 Percent." Source: http://wearethe99percent .tumblr.com/.

country who do not actually work. According to this meme, the 99 percent protesters have failed to take personal responsibility for their actions. This dialogue between the "99" and "53," alongside their numerous offspring (e.g., the "1 percent"), constituted, according to Ryan Milner, a rich sphere of multivoiced meme-based discussion.

For the sake of clarity, I have so far differentiated between memes as dealing with persuasion, action, or discussion. Yet my brief analysis has demonstrated that in reality these functions are intertwined: *political memes are often used as an amalgamation of all three.* The 99 percent meme, for instance, was created as part of a grassroots movement; it was meant to be persuasive and it ignited a rich and diverse meme-based discourse.

Not all Occupy memes were as serious as the 99 percent meme. Many others drew on vast arenas of pop culture to create comic effects. Building on Henry Jenkins's work on these new, playful dimensions of civic participation, Ryan Milner and Geniesa Tay show how pop culture is used in memes as a common ground to discuss politics.[11] As pop culture is part of people's everyday lives and cultural identities, using it to talk about politics makes the latter more approachable. Pop culture thus serves as a platform through which individuals can communicate with each other about politics in a playful and engaging way. For example, Tay describes the heavy usage of *Star Wars* characters in memes as shorthand to communicate meaning.

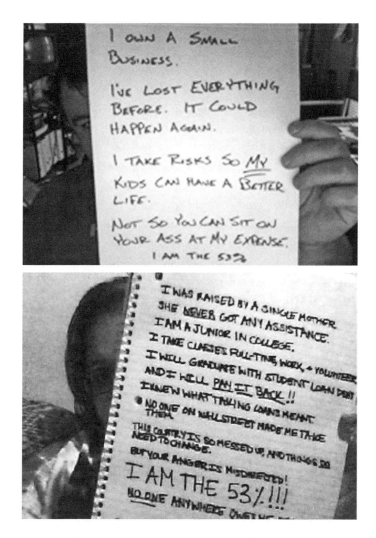

Figure 15 "We Are the 53 Percent." Source: http://the53.tumblr.com/.

When a public figure is framed as a Jedi Knight, it is quite clear that he or she is on the good side of the force, with the opposite applying to any politician associated with the Imperial forces. In figure 16, a popular accusation that Occupy protesters have only a vague plan of action is turned on its head when uttered by Palpatine, while protesters are associated with the positive characters of Yoda and Luke Skywalker. Yet, as demonstrated in chapter 4, this heavy reliance on pop culture images in political memes may, at some points, lead to a process of "depoliticization," in which the political and critical aspects of Internet memes are diminished in favor of pure playful amusement.

Political Memetic Photos

As demonstrated in the analysis of the "Pepper-Spraying Cop" meme in chapter 3, meme-based political discourse often begins with a single "memetic photo" that relates to political actors and controversies. In order to find shared attributes of such photos, I analyzed an array of examples from the United States, France, China, Israel, and Egypt (assembled through the method described in chapter 6). I found that most political memetic photos relate to a single

Figure 16 "Occupy *Star Wars*." Source: http://www.tumblr.com/tagged/occupy%20star%20wars.

MAY THE EXCESSIVE FORCE BE WITH YOU

theme: *an interplay between the "frontstage" and "backstage" of political performances.* Described by sociologist Erving Goffman back in the 1950s, "frontstage" is the main site in which impression management activities are performed.[12] Such activities are carried out in front of an audience, aiming to project a desired image such as "I am a devoted and strong politician, who sticks by his principles." In contrast, "backstage" is a more private area, where intimacy, familiarity, and authenticity govern. Far from the public eye, this is also the place where the techniques of impression management are practiced.

The disintegration of the borderline between front- and backstage regions stands at the core of many political scandals in the twentieth century. In instances such as the Clinton–Lewinsky scandal or Watergate, something said or done in the supposedly safe backstage realm leaked into the frontstage of newspapers and newscasts. As a result, embarrassed politicians were required to apologize for actions taken behind the scenes.[13] Surprisingly, this mode of breaching the screen between front- and backstage is quite rare in memetic photos. What we find instead is a different sort of blend between the two spheres: *a carefully articulated, strategic exposure of a political backstage, presented frontstage.* Prominent examples of this category include the photograph taken in the Situation Room of the White House, picturing President Barack Obama alongside members of the National Security team receiving an update on Osama bin Laden's assassination in Pakistan, and the Netanyahu–Shalit photo, featuring Israeli Prime Minister Benjamin Netanyahu smiling proudly in the background while Gilad Shalit, the Israeli soldier released after five years of captivity by Hamas, embraces his father for the first time.

In their memetic responses to such photos, users expose them as "inauthentic," flawed, and manipulated. For instance, the meme developing in response to the Netanyahu–Shalit photo has been tagged as "Bibi Gump": it situates Netanyahu in a gallery of historic events, taking credit for the 1969 moon landing, Maccabi Tel Aviv's 1977 European Cup basketball victory, the signing of the peace treaty with Egypt in 1979, and the royal wedding of Prince William and Kate Middleton. In this case and others, netizens use memes to articulate a collective critical response toward what they perceive as slick manipulation by a politician.

Similar responses emerge when Internet users discover that a seemingly authentic "backstage" photo was artificially constructed. In the case of the "Sarkozy Was There" meme, a photo of Nicolas Sarkozy at the Berlin Wall was uploaded to his Facebook page, with the claim that it was taken on the evening East German officials opened the gates to the West. Yet, according to "Know Your Meme," shortly afterward the French media showed that Sarkozy was indeed in the right place, but not at the right time:

the photo had been taken a week after the historical moment. A slightly different kind of fabrication was ridiculed in the case of the "Three Chinese Officials" meme. It all began when a Chinese government website of Huili County published a photo showing three local officials inspecting a newly completed road. The only problem was that the photo looked like a badly produced Photoshop paste-up: the officials seemed to be levitating several inches above the ground. The photo generated many mocking memetic responses, in which the officials were relocated in other contexts. As a result, the website issued an apology, explaining that the three men did visit the road in question, but the photographer felt his original pictures were not impressive enough and relocated the officials.

Users' memetic responses to such manipulations of political images can be seen as the bottom-up, digital incarnations of Jon Stewart and Stephen Colbert's agendas in *The Daily Show* and *The Colbert Report*. These shows continuously reveal the "backstage" strategies that politicians and reporters use in order to sound persuasive and authoritative, even when they do not have much to say.[14] Henry Jenkins claims that such programs provide "good training grounds for monitorial citizens," who become accustomed to looking out for signs of manipulation and fabrication.[15] By manipulating political photos, users signal that they

Figure 17   The "Bibi Gump" meme. Source: http://fuckyeahbibibomb .tumblr.com/.

are aware of the artificial construction of images and that they can create competing (and somewhat less flattering) images themselves.

Memes thus expand the range of participatory options in democracies: citizens can express their political opinions in new and accessible ways, engage in heated debates, and enjoy the process to boot. But in nondemocracies, Internet memes are not just about expanding discursive opportunities—they may represent the idea of democracy itself.

Memes as Democratic Subversion: The Case of China

Over the last decade, the Internet has become an important arena for public discourse in China. The immensity and anonymity characterizing new media offer millions of Chinese Internet users a new promise of freer information. And indeed, since its early days, political discourse and attempts at political protest have flourished in Chinese cyberspace. Aware of the dangers this kind of subversive communication could pose to the regime, the Chinese government has been implementing an active censorship system, including blocking certain keyword searches and websites; monitoring chat rooms, blogs, and microblogging platforms; and requiring the installation of censorship software on new computers. It also promotes self-censorship, obliging administrators of chat rooms, for instance, to remove potentially objectionable content. Recently the government justified such censorship as part of the endeavor to build a "harmonious society." The concept is associated with China's current president, Hu Jintao, who uses it to describe the need for a socialist unified society in an age of transition.

This policy generated many forms of resistance. For instance, Christopher Rea describes netizens who sarcastically complain about "being harmonized" after their blogs or chat rooms have been closed by government censors. This ironic usage led to the word being flagged as a sensitive keyword, which puts those who use it on their websites at risk. In response, bloggers and other content creators switched the characters making up the word to produce another phrase with a slightly different intonation. This resulted in a pun, as the new phrase means "river crab." Thus, when bloggers write about "river crab," or being "river crabbed," they are actually talking about censorship. This in turn soon spawned popular visual memes.[16] In one, a crab is wearing three watches, a pun on the "three represents," declared by Jiang Zemin in 2000: "The Party must always represent the requirements of the development of China's advanced productive forces, the orientation of the development of China's advanced culture, and the fundamental interests of the overwhelming majority of the people in China."[17]

The "River Crab" meme was also manifest in video clips. For instance, in one of these videos, dubbed with a boys band pop soundtrack, televised footage of government meetings and embarrassing photos of the president are re-edited to include flashes of watch-wearing crabs. The resonance between some of the images and the song's lyrics (for instance, a photo of Jiang combing his hair is synchronized with the words "prettyin' up") denigrates Chinese leaders in a way that would never appear in local mass media.[18]

Another popular Chinese political meme that was initially constructed to manipulate the censors is the "Grass Mud Horse." It evolved as a response to the authorities' campaign to cleanse the Internet of pornographic content, banned as unhealthy and harmful to Chinese youth. While such "purifying" actions ostensibly focused on sexual content, in reality they were used to silence unapproved political opinions. This led to the creation of the "Grass Mud Horse"—a "mythical beast" whose name in Chinese is pronounced as literally meaning "fuck your mother." Galloping onto the Internet in 2008, Grass Mud Horse became an instant memetic hit. Christopher Rea describes the video that introduced this animal to the world as "a jaunty ditty sung by a chorus of childish voices," paired with moving images of peaceful alpacas. Yet this sweet and innocent facade is deceiving. What makes the song funny is the incongruity between how its lyrics are meant to be read (by the censors) and how they sound. For instance, the line "On

Figure 18   The "River Crab" meme. Source: http://chinadigitaltimes
.net/2012/03/word-of-the-week-river-crab/.

the vast and beautiful Male Gobi desert is a herd of grass mud horses" actually sounds like "In your mother's vast and beautiful cunt is a group fucking your mother." Later in the song the grass mud horses defeat the dangerous river crabs, protecting their grassland. In this encrypted narrative, the harmless beasts represent innocent Internet users, who are victims of a cruel censorship regime, but will prevail. The Grass Mud Horse song has inspired numerous memetic responses. In 2009 and onward a flow of cartoon versions, Photoshop reactions, and poems have swamped Chinese websites, generating interest and coverage of the phenomena in other countries as well.

Yet this story does not end in cyberspace. Shaojung Sharon Wang describes a process through which this subversive symbol—created in coded language as a new form of social resistance—has been commercialized.[19] As early as 2009, the popularity of the creature resulted in a stream of merchandise, such as T-shirts and soft toys sold by Internet retailers and in toy stores. In a sense, this move from cyberspace to physical artifacts in the "real world" represents Internet users' urge to deepen their shared subversive experience. At the same time, the process also signifies the power of capitalism to reinvent itself: as Wang says, "With the productive and participatory aspects of internet tools, the products have already ensured a profit because through free advertising, internet users act voluntarily as marketers."[20]

So what is the meaning of memes in such tightly controlled political environments? In these contexts, political memes seem to be more than just a ventilation of anger and frustration; the widespread subversive meme circulation serves as a powerful public display of criticism and distrust. It breaks the facade of optimism and unity presented in official mass media, showing that things are not as "harmonious" as the party would like to present them. Nonetheless, it is still unclear whether this public criticism will be translated to connective action and actual regime change.

In this chapter, I have provided a snapshot of contemporary political memes in democratic and nondemocratic settings. To conclude, I will take a step back and compare Internet memes with predigital memes, such as political jokes in the former Soviet Union. Memes have always played an important role as venues for expressing opinions and subverting established order, and in this fundamental sense there is nothing new in their latest digital incarnation. Yet whereas in the predigital era political memes were mostly part of the private lives of ordinary people who were ranting against those in power, in the digital era these expressions have become part of the public sphere: a performative display of opinions that is meant to be heard far and wide. Moreover, as demonstrated by Ryan Milner, since meme hubs such as 4chan and Reddit incorporate a variety of contrasting voices and opinions, Internet memes assume a new role in deliberative processes, providing a polyvocal "meeting space" between opposing camps. In this sense, they differ from political jokes, often told in intimate gatherings with like-minded others.

A further realm of difference between old and new political memes relates to form: digital memes are much more visual than their predecessors. This has two main implications. First, visual display allows greater integration between politics and pop culture. While it may take some ingenuity to invent a verbal joke in which Barack Obama meets Luke Skywalker, it is easy to Photoshop the president's head on a Jedi's body. A second implication of the visual nature of Internet memes relates to their polysemic potential—that is, their tendency to be open to multiple readings. Whereas in verbal jokes the target of mockery and its scorned feature are often clear, visual images' openness and lack of a clear narrative may invoke contrasting interpretations. Lillian Boxman-Shabtai claims that this potential for multiple meanings is stronger when visual imagery involves intertextuality: the additional layer of meanings associated with a text such as *Star Wars* may add complexity and ambiguity to the message.[21] Thus, whereas one person will read the Obama-as-Luke meme as glorifying Obama, another will understand it as criticizing this leader's prevalent construction as a superhero. Yet in both cases, the Force is with Internet users: as demonstrated in this chapter, Internet memes constitute a new arena of political discourse and, possibly, of bottom-up political influence.

WHEN INTERNET MEMES GO GLOBAL

So far, we have looked at memes as embedded in local cultures and power structures. But Internet memes are rarely confined to a single geographic location. Probably more than any previous medium, the Internet is suited to cross-national large-scale meme distribution. The realization of this potential, however, is not determined merely by technology; rather, it is the complex nexus of Internet users' practices and choices that generates modes of globalization. In this chapter, I will show that in the last decade Internet memes have indeed become powerful—yet often invisible—agents of globalization. But this is not a one-way process of cultural homogenization: at the same time, modified versions of imported meme formulas stress the uniqueness of local cultures. After charting some basic definitions and controversies related to globalization, I will look into two modes of meme-based global diffusion: those related to verbal memes and those associated with visual and audiovisual content.

According to one of its numerous definitions, globalization is the "developing process of complex interconnections between societies, cultures, institutions and individuals worldwide."[1] Although regional and worldwide interdependences are old phenomena, the speed and scale of global flows has accelerated dramatically in recent decades, affecting almost every aspect of social life. Since the 1990s, the rapid growth of the Internet has raised new hopes, anxieties, and debates about globalization. Built as an international network of networks, the Internet allows—technically at least—the effortless transcending of national borders. However, a growing body of research suggests that contrary to the predicted obliteration of space and distance in a new digitized order, cyberspace is embedded in—and shaped by—material, social, linguistic, and cultural contexts.[2]

The debate over globalization—both in the predigital and digital eras—is tied to a large extent to the claim that global flows have a specific direction, from "the West to the rest." Globalization, according to its critics, is a form of Western imperialism, serving the economic, cultural, and political interests of the West in general and the United States in particular. This description of globalization as an inevitable, one-way, monolithic Americanization process has been widely challenged. Coined by Roland Robertson, the term "glocalization" was borrowed from Japanese business circles to portray the "processes that telescope

In the last decade Internet memes have indeed become powerful—yet often invisible—agents of globalization.

the global and local (scales) to make a blend."[3] The concept challenges the sharp distinction between cultural homogenization and heterogenization by depicting contemporary culture as synthesizing internal and external influences. Thus, rather than simply accepting or rejecting global models, local actors combine the foreign and the familiar to create multifaceted, hybrid cultures.

These disputes over globalization and glocalization are evident in contemporary research into the flow of Internet content. Some studies of globalization and the Internet support the arguments about inequality and Americanization, highlighting both global divides in infrastructure and access, as well as Western-American biases in aspects such as language, commodification, and commercialization processes.[4] Parallel to these findings, a growing body of literature also provides evidence for processes of local and glocal Internet uses. These studies show that many people use the Internet locally to communicate with people and institutions in their own country or region.

A major focus in such user-oriented studies is language: from its early days, the lingua franca of the Internet has been English, evoking concerns about the medium's role in promoting "linguistic imperialism" and threatening the status of smaller languages. Yet recent studies indicate that the dominance of English is declining. As early as 2003, two-thirds of Internet users across the globe were not native speakers of English, and the accelerating growth of Internet use in countries such as China was expected to strengthen this trend.[5] This linguistic variation invokes a series of fundamental questions about cultural globalization and the Internet: How can the Internet facilitate global flows in a multilingual setting? What is the function of translation in this environment? To what extent is globalization in such a context based on visual cues? And finally, what is the role of ordinary Internet users in these new processes of globalization?

In what follows, I will explore some of these questions through the prism of *user-generated globalization*—a process in which memes are translated, customized, and distributed across the globe by ordinary Internet users. User-generated globalization has previously gone unnoticed in the research literature for three reasons: first, it is not driven by high-profile commercial agencies, such as major production companies, but by the daily practice of many ordinary users; second, unlike the transnational flow of mass media content (such as TV formats), this arena of globalization does not explicitly involve commerce; and finally, once a text is translated and some local markers are added, its foreign origins may be invisible to those who read and distribute it.

My colleagues and I explored the scale and scope of user-generated globalization through two consecutive studies that focused on the translation of verbal jokes. In the first one (conducted in collaboration with Mike

Thelwall), we looked into the narrow case of one Internet joke about men, women, and computers.[6] Framed as a letter from a frustrated computer user to a tech support team, the text focuses on the agonies of "Upgrading from Girlfriend 7.0 to Wife 1.0." The user complains that Wife 1.0 has "begun unexpected child processing that took up a lot of space and valuable resources," and that it blocks applications such as "Poker Night 10.3, Football 5.0, Hunting and Fishing 7.5, and Racing 3.6." In his response, the tech support representative explains that the user's problems stem from "a primary misconception: many people upgrade from Girlfriend 7.0 to Wife 1.0, thinking it is merely a utilities and entertainment program. Wife 1.0 is an OPERATING SYSTEM and is designed by its creator to run EVERYTHING!!!" While this version is ostensibly from a masculine perspective, a feminine version of this text has also become widespread over the Web. In "Upgrading from Boyfriend 7.0 to Husband 1.0," the newly wedded wife complains that "Husband 1.0" severely limits "access to wardrobe, flower and jewelry applications," which "functioned flawlessly under Boyfriend 7.0," and that it "un-installed many other valuable programs" such as "Romance 9.5" and "Personal Attention 6.5."

We found this joke to be highly popular in English, and anticipated that its topics—computers and romantic love—would appeal to people worldwide. Our aim was therefore to explore the extent to which it was translated into other languages. We looked for copies of translated versions in the top nine (non-English) languages spoken by Internet users when the study was carried out (2009): Chinese, Spanish, Japanese, French, German, Portuguese, Arabic, Korean, and Italian. We found that the joke traveled well across linguistic and cultural borders: it appeared in a considerable number of copies in eight out of the nine languages examined.

The strong global aspect of the joke's diffusion was accompanied by a limited degree of glocalization; translations in the three languages explored in detail—Chinese, German, and Portuguese—incorporated many small local adaptations. Thus, for instance, in the German translations many changes related to sports-oriented references: NBA and rugby were replaced by German indicators such as *Fussball-Bundesliga* (the German premier league soccer) and *Sportschau* (a major German soccer TV show). Yet although the "flavors" in these languages differed, the "ingredients"—in our case, postfeminist assumptions and gender-related stereotypes—remained unchanged. Throughout the globe, "Mars and Venus"–related stereotypes of needy women who are too talkative and emotional and men who just want to be left alone to watch their sports were replicated time and again without significant opposition.[7]

Out of the nine languages examined in the study, the only one in which translated texts for the joke were very rare was Arabic. A possible explanation may be culture-related: some of the norms encoded in the joke—such as premarital sexual relationships—may be considered unsuitable in Arab-speaking societies. This explanation was corroborated about a year after we finished our data collection, when a new, Arabic version of the joke started to propagate quickly on the Web. The joke was reframed as a letter written by a woman to her husband, who is a computer programmer. While built on the same comic mechanism of juxtaposing marriage life and computers, it does not include hints at premarital sex and is saturated with references to Islamic customs.

The major limitation of our first investigation was its focus on a single case study: it was impossible to draw general conclusions on the basis of one joke. In a more recent study, conducted by Hadar Levy, Mike Thelwall, and myself, we significantly expanded the scope of analysis, tracing the translations of 100 popular jokes in English to the top languages spoken by Internet users in 2010 (Chinese, Spanish, Japanese, French, German, Portuguese, Arabic, Korean, and Russian). We found that *user-generated globalization* through joke translation is common but varies greatly across languages. While many translated joke copies were found in five languages (Russian, Portuguese, Spanish, French, German), fewer copies were found in Chinese and Arabic, and significantly fewer in Korean and Japanese. The results may be related to cultural proximity:

The top languages on the list are spoken in so-called Western cultures based mainly in America or Europe, while the languages in which we found fewer translations are prevalent mainly in Asia and Africa. We also found significant differences between various jokes in terms of global spread: while some jokes circulate widely across the globe, others are "translation resistant" and appear only in English.[8] "Global" jokes shared two main topics: gender differences and consumerism. These two themes are strongly manifest in the following example, found in many languages:

It's not difficult to make a woman happy. A man only needs to be:

1. a friend
2. a companion
3. a lover
4. a brother
5. a father
6. a master
7. a chef
8. an electrician
9. a carpenter
10. a plumber
11. a mechanic
12. a decorator
13. a stylist

(and the list continues until clause 44)

WITHOUT FORGETTING TO:

    45. give her compliments regularly

    46. love shopping

    47. be honest

    48. be very rich

    49. not stress her out

    50. not look at other girls

AND AT THE SAME TIME, YOU MUST ALSO:

    51. give her lots of attention, but expect little yourself

    52. give her lots of time, especially time for herself

    53. give her lots of space, never worrying about where she goes

IT IS VERY IMPORTANT:

    54. Never to forget:

    * birthdays

    * anniversaries

    * arrangements she makes

HOW TO MAKE A MAN HAPPY

    1. Show up naked

    2. Bring alcohol

"Global" jokes tend not to mention specific places or companies, and if they do, they focus on high-profile corporations or products, such as Microsoft or Barbie. In contrast, translation-resistant jokes tend to focus on specific places within America, on local American stereotypes (for example, rednecks), and on local American politics. Overall, our findings suggest that Internet jokes serve as powerful and invisible agents of Westernization and Americanization; yet this is not a universal process: some cultures (in particular Korean and Japanese) do not seem to participate in cultural globalization through joke diffusion.

So far, I have discussed only one mode of user-generated globalization – the circulation of verbal humor. But the process of international meme diffusion is not confined to verbal forms: in fact, visual content may cross linguistic and national borders with much greater ease. Research has not yet addressed this issue systematically, but a growing body of examples suggests that flows of visual content are taking place, and in considerable volumes. Similar to verbal humor, visual and audiovisual humor forms are often subject to localization strategies. I will discuss these glocalization processes with reference to two cases: the migration of the "Successful Black Man" meme to the Holy Land and international versions of "Gangnam Style."

The "Successful Black Man" meme features a photo of a young black man dressed in a suit, accompanied by two captions: the top line hints at a (usually negative) stereotype associated with being black, while the bottom one reverses it to display a middle-class, responsible family man. For instance, in the examples below, the initial line "Let's all get high" (hinting at the stereotypical association of blacks and drugs) is reversed by "grades on our finals," "Just got outta jail" turns out to be part of a family Monopoly game, and "I jacked that lady's car" proves to be nothing but the first step of a gentleman changing a stranger's flat tire. The humorous effect of this meme derives from the comic clash between two scripts:[9] a false one that adheres to stereotypic conventions and the true one in which the stereotypes prove false.

Ryan Milner discusses the ambiguous social implications of this meme.[10] On the one hand, its name, "Successful Black Man," hints at the racial presumption that the modifier "successful" needs to be inserted before the "black man" category in order to differentiate between this guy and the "regular" black man. The meme thus reinforces stereotypes by presenting the exception that proves the rule. Yet at the same time, this meme is poignant with a strong anti-stereotyping message: It challenges readers' (often invisible) racist assumptions by presenting a counterexample to each of them. The second clause can thus be read as "punishing" readers for their initial stereotypical reading.

Similarly to other prominent memes, "Successful Black Man" has migrated from the United States into other national settings. In some of them, it has been altered in order to make a better fit with local culture. In Israel, for

Figure 19 "Successful Black Man." Source: http://www.quickmeme.com/.

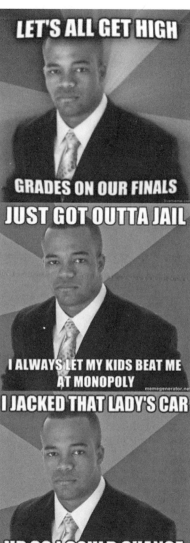

example, it has been reincarnated in memes about the ultra-Orthodox Jews (*Haredim*) and the settlers in the West Bank (*Mitnachalim*). The meme "Akiva, the Humanist Ultra-Orthodox Man" replicates the comic mechanism underpinning its American ancestor: it comprises a top line which alludes at a stereotype strongly associated with the Ultra-Orthodox group, juxtaposed with a bottom line that turns the stereotype on its head. In the examples below, the cry "Woman, to the kitchen" (hinting at strict and segregating gender roles in this society) turns into the surprising: "you need to taste the kartoffel that I made you," and the assertion "In our house we never watch movies" (hinting at the Haredi ban on television and films) is followed by the contrasting modifier: "that are of lower quality than DVD-RIP."

At first glance, the Israeli version of "Successful Black Man" seems to work similarly to the original American meme as it simultaneously confirms and subverts stereotypes. But a closer look reveals that this is not the case. By tagging a name to the character, the meme conveys the message that we are talking about a singular exception that actually validates the stereotypical assumptions associated with the group. In other words: the meme tells us that only one specific Haredi is humanistic; the rest are not. Moreover, since people who encounter this meme are often familiar with the original "Successful Black Man" meme, they may interpret it not as a reflection on Israeli

Figure 20 "Akiva, the Humanist Ultra-Orthodox Man." Source: http://www.10gag.co.il/.

society, but as a playful parody on the American origin. Thus, the strong satirical aspect embedded in the original meme seems to get lost in translation. This example demonstrates that dividing memes to form, content and stance may be useful in understanding mechanisms of localization: While the Israeli version copied the format of the American meme, it altered its content and satirical stance.

A more recent example of widespread local adaptations of an Internet meme is that of the music video "Gangnam Style." In chapter 6, I attributed this video's memetic appeal to a combination of simple, repetitive, elements and content that seems (to most non-Korean viewers) completely whimsical and full of puzzling elements. This combination allows, on the one hand, easy imitation of some of the video's basic features (such as the horse dance and the recurring expressions), and on the other, incorporation of a very wide arena of themes and topics to its derivatives.

And indeed, "Gangnam Style" has produced an astounding volume of derivative videos, spanning almost every possible language and nationality. Given the great variety of contexts in which these derivatives were produced, it is striking to see the similarities in the ways users across the globe have reacted to the video. In particular, they have tended to charge the clip with local meaning by replacing the word "Gangnam"—which, as previously noted, refers to an affluent neighborhood in Seoul—with a variety of substitute terms such as "Mexi Style," "Romney Style," and "Aussie Battler Style." This wide array of adaptations stems from the connotative richness of the word "style," which has been described by Penelope Eckert as the "visible manifestation of social meanings." Style is regarded in both academic and popular discourses as a pivotal aspect of the construction and maintenance of personal and collective identities.[11] The various adaptations of the clip seem to relate to four distinct styles, or identity circles.

The first and most notable identity circle relates to style as an expression of national, regional, or subcultural identities. Some of these clips seem to be directed outward, using the video as a means of attracting visitors. Such clips are either in English or have English subtitles. For instance, the creators of "Orang Sabah Style" explain: "Sabah is one of the states of Malaysia. It is simply a beautiful place. Everyone can come and visit Sabah for tourism spot." Others seem to use it in a more internal way, almost as a private joke. For instance, a group of young Saudis produced a version that includes a sarcastic reference to the phenomenon of young men wearing white undershirts and thobe pants that look more like undergarments, both when they are home and outside, a phenomenon that triggers complaints from their wives.[12] Other "internal" videos relate to subgroups within national settings. Thus, for instance, the lyrics of "Aussie Battler Style" replace the line "Hey, sexy lady" with "Hey, chips and gravy," or "Hey, we love Lowndesy" (referring to the famous Australian racing driver Craig Lowndes).

Alongside those videos that follow the original clip in a depiction of a particular place, others have followed a different attribute of the original video, namely, its construction as social satire. Some of the most viewed clips from across the world build on the song's popularity to convey straightforward political messages. For instance, the American "Mitt Romney Style," produced in the course of the presidential election campaign, depicts the Republican candidate as a rich and corrupt politician, who's "got distinguished hair and a private jet that flies me way up in the air." In China, a version entitled "Grass Mud Horse Style" (referring to the anti-censorship symbol discussed in chapter 8) has been removed from local websites by government authorities. This version featured its creator—the Chinese artist and political activist Ai Weiwei—dancing to the sounds of the original song with a pair of handcuffs that symbolize his arrest by Chinese authorities in 2011.

If political clips use the video's popularity to display controversial points of view, "institutional" clips tend to build on it mainly for self-promotion. For instance, "NASA Johnson Style"—a parody created by no less than the American National Aeronautics and Space Administration—valorizes the cutting-edge technologies and scientific work involved in sending astronauts to space. Similar promotion strategies have been used by a wide array of organizations across the globe. In France, for example, a team working in a certain nightclub in the Bordeaux region remade the video and posted it as an explicit commercial.

Finally, the video has been used for presenting a wide range of personal styles, which are often created for ceremonial events. People have remade the clip for display at weddings, bar mitzvahs, and Christmas parties. While some of these versions use the song as a "hook" on which to hang lyrics depicting a specific individual's personal style (for example, "Jacob's Style"), the main mechanism for personalizing the general template in most of them is shooting the clip in vernacular and other familiar locations, using the event's hosts and guests as the main protagonists. In such cases, the popularity of the original video serves as a common denominator between the various guests attending the event, connecting them to each other through the pop culture world they inhabit.

This last point leads to a more general assertion about the social and cultural role of "local" meme remakes in a globalized world. In chapter 3, I discussed the key role memes play in a society based on networked individualism. I argued that, on the one hand, each memetic version is unique, reflecting the digital literacy and creativity of its producers; on the other hand, adding one's version of a well-known clip or template signals membership in a larger community that enjoys similar (pop) culture artifacts. This community is construed simultaneously as global and local: the vernacular versions of "Gangnam Style" use the universal/Western template of dance movements and rapid editing to strip the video from its original (local Korean) context and charge it with a different, culture-specific meaning. Thus, if globalization is invisible in the case of translated verbal jokes, the story of transnational flows is manifested explicitly in memetic videos such as "Gangnam Style."

FUTURE DIRECTIONS FOR INTERNET MEME RESEARCH

If you've made it to the last chapter of this book, I hope I have convinced you that:

(1) The veteran term "meme" is highly relevant and ap plicable for understanding a wide range of contemporary behaviors, ranging from worldwide political protests to bizarre Korean dance movements.

(2) By defining Internet memes not as single units that propagate well but as groups of items with similar characteristics, we can study memes as reflections of cultural and social collectives, as well as the individual voices constituting them.

(3) The terms "viral" and "memetic" are not coextensive: the features that lead us to share a certain video or photo differ from the features that drive us to mimic or remix it.

(4) Internet memes play a key role in contemporary formulations of political participation and cultural globalization.

These four points merge into a single assertion: we need to take Internet memes seriously. The fledgling field of research devoted to this understanding has already demonstrated that Internet memes may help us decipher contemporary political, cultural, and social processes. In this short book, I have traced some of the main trends in the field, but I have not been able to cover the entire range of possible implications of this multifarious topic. Therefore, by way of conclusion, I wish to highlight four promising areas for meme research.

- *The politics of memetic participation*   Memes do not just flow on the Internet in a capricious, arbitrary manner. Behind each successful meme is a person—or rather, many people. Understanding the individuals who participate in the process of generating and diffusing Internet memes, and finding out how their participation patterns relate to race, ethnicity, gender, and power, is a worthwhile endeavor. For instance, Noam Gal's work on "It Gets Better" (discussed in chapter 4) showed that even in a campaign energized by the liberal motto of supporting gay teenagers, the majority of presenters were white, young males. Further work, spanning a wider range of case studies, would help us discover to what extent Internet memes do indeed serve as alternative routes of expression for marginalized groups, and to what extent they reflect well-entrenched power structures.

- *Internet memes as a language*   As elaborated in chapter 7, the past decade has been marked not only by the explosion of Internet memes, but also by their evolution into distinct formulas. Because memes constitute shared spheres of cultural knowledge, they allow us to convey complex ideas within a short phrase or image. Thus, instead of saying "I had a bad date and I feel miserable and lonely," one can simply paste the "Forever Alone" character.

This influx of shared symbols has led to the evolution of memes into a secondary layer of language, often complementing and sometimes even replacing its standard uses. According to Ryan Milner, in order to use this memetic language correctly, one needs a certain familiarity with subcultural standards.[1] The "right" or "wrong" way of employing memes in a discourse is never definitive—it is negotiated through continuous intergroup discussions within each "meme hub." Asaf Nissenboim, who studied memetic practices in 4chan, found that appropriate meme use has become a form of cultural capital in this setting, differentiating between those who are "in the know" and are thus part of the community and those who are outsiders.[2]

If indeed memes are evolving as "the language of the Internet," future research should take on the ambitious mission of understanding how this language is used by diverse groups. One of the main questions relating to this process has to do with global and local identities: to what extent do Internet memes constitute a "global" language mastered by billions of netizens, and to what extent do specific cultures create their own discrete memetic vernaculars?

- *Memes and political change* In chapter 8, I offered an overview of the ways in which Internet memes are used as modes of political participation by citizens in democratic and nondemocratic countries. But while memetic activities empower citizens to express political opinions in new and creative ways, the extent to which memes actually influence political processes such as legislation or regime change remains unclear. For instance, although Occupy Wall Street was definitely a memetic success, it has failed to dent the status quo, let alone generate the economic and political transformation it advocated. Future research could thus delve into the question of what constitutes an Internet meme's "effect," and how this effect can be measured.

- *Viral and memetic success* In chapter 6, I charted some factors that enhance viral success (that is, the probability that people will share a certain item), differentiating them from factors that enhance memetic success (that is, the probability that people will respond creatively to an item by remaking or remixing it). This distinction may have practical implications for advertisers and other professionals who aim at maximizing the effects of their messages. While currently the buzzword in the advertising industry is "viral," understanding the power of the memetic seems to be important in an era of growing user engagement. As argued in chapter 6, memetic videos compete well in contemporary attention economies, since each derivative strengthens the status of the original viral video, while at the same time the initial viral video helps promote its derivatives. Yet the map of factors that I charted in chapter 6 as augmenting mimesis and virality is only a first step in a long journey: presented as an overarching general model, it misses the more nuanced factors that may apply to specific genres and settings. Future research should therefore look into distinctive factors enhancing virality and memetic uptake in specific genres, such as commercial advertising or political campaigns.

As is evident in this concluding chapter, there are considerably more question marks than exclamation points in the state of our knowledge of Internet memes. But this should not deter us. Since memes are fundamental building blocks of digital culture, understanding them means understanding ourselves. A comprehensive tapestry of the ways in which memes interact with social, cultural, and political realities will require a combination of quantitative "big data" analysis and qualitative close reading of texts, as well as comparative cross-cultural studies. Hopefully, these challenges will be met by enthusiastic researchers, blessed with a tad of humor.

GLOSSARY

Internet meme   (a) A group of digital content units sharing common characteristics of content, form, and/or stance. For instance—photos featuring funny cats with captions share a topic (cats), form (photo + caption), and stance (humor). (b) These units are created with awareness of each other—the person posting the "cat with caption" image builds on the previous cats in the series. (c) These units are circulated, imitated, and/or transformed via the Internet by many users. Internet memes are multiparticipant creative expressions through which cultural and political identities are communicated and negotiated.

Meme   A term introduced by the biologist Richard Dawkins in his 1976 book *The Selfish Gene*. Dawkins defined memes as small cultural units of transmission, analogous to genes, which are spread from person to person by copying or imitation. Examples of memes in his pioneering essay include cultural artifacts such as melodies, catchphrases, and clothing fashions, as well as abstract beliefs. Like genes, memes are defined as replicators that undergo variation, competition, selection, and retention. At any given moment, many memes are competing for the attention of hosts; however, only memes suited to their sociocultural environment spread successfully, while others become extinct.

Virality   A diffusion process in which a certain message (such as a catchphrase, video, or image) spreads from one person to another via digital and social media platforms. The process is characterized by great speed (the number of people exposed to the "viral" message increases dramatically in a short time), and with broad reach (achieved by bridging multiple networks). The propagated message is often defined as "viral content" (e.g., "viral video"). When viral content lures user-created derivatives in the form of re-mix or imitation, it can be described as "memetic."

Prevalent Meme Hubs

4chan An imageboard website on which users upload and discuss visual images. It is divided into multiple channels, or boards, with particular content and guidelines. The most popular board is "random" (also known as "/b/"), which is notorious for its wild, aggressive, and often rude style and content. Memes constitute an important facet of 4chan, serving as an integral part of many discussions. 4chan is also a major hub of the hacktivist group Anonymous. See http://4chan.com/.

Tumblr A microblogging platform on which users upload short posts to a profile known as a tumblog. Tumblr also functions as a social networking site, in which Tumblrs "follow" each other. Most posts are constituted of images, many of which can be defined as memes. See http://www.tumblr.com.

Reddit A content aggregation site that consists of user-generated news links. These links are voted up-or-down by the community members, tagged as "redditors." It contains subreddits—boards dedicated to various topics. It is known as a "lefty" or "geeky" hub of Internet culture and memes. See http://www.reddit.com/.

NOTES

Chapter 2

1. Richard Dawkins, *The Selfish Gene* (Oxford: Oxford University Press, 1976); Susan Blackmore, *The Meme Machine* (Oxford: Oxford University Press, 1999); Hans-Cees Speel, "Memetics: On a Conceptual Framework for Cultural Evolution," in *The Evolution of Complexity*, ed. Francis Heylighen and Diederik Aerts (Dordrecht: Kluwer, 1996).

2. For elaboration on the term "meme" and its origins, see David L. Hull, "Taking Memetics Seriously: Memetics Will Be What We Make It," in *Darwinizing Culture: The Status of Memetics as a Science*, ed. Robert Aunger (Oxford: Oxford University Press, 2000), 43–168.

3. In *Encyclopedia of Complexity and System Sciences*, ed. Robert A. Meyers (New York: Springer, 2009), http://pespmc1.vub.ac.be/Papers/Memetics-Springer.pdf.

4. Henry Jenkins, Xiaochang Li, Ana Domb Krauskopf, and Joshua Green, "If It Doesn't Spread, It's Dead (Part One): Media Viruses and Memes," Feb. 11, 2009, http://henryjenkins.org/2009/02/if_it_doesnt_spread_its_dead_p.html.

5. Rosaria Conte, "Memes Through (Social) Minds," in *Darwinizing Culture: The Status of Memetics as a Science*, ed. Robert Aunger (Oxford: Oxford University Press, 2000), 83–120.

6. Colin Lankshear and Michele Knobel, *A New Literacies Sampler* (New York: Peter Lang, 2007).

7. On memes as folklore, see Lynne McNeill, "The End of the Internet: A Folk Response to the Provision of Infinite Choice," in *Folklore and the Internet*, ed. Trevor J. Blank (Logan: Utah University Press, 2009), 80–97.

Chapter 3

1. One of the first accounts of the intersection between memes and the Internet can be found in Francis Heylighen and Klaas Chielens, "Cultural Evolution and Memetics," in *Encyclopedia of Complexity and System Science*, ed. Robert A. Meyers, http://pespmc1.vub.ac.be/Papers/Memetics-Springer.pdf.

2. Nicholas John, "Sharing and Web 2.0: The Emergence of a Keyword," *New Media and Society* (published online before print, July 3, 2012, doi:

10.1177/14614448124506). See also Nicholas John, "The Social Logics of Sharing," *Communication Review* (forthcoming).

3. Daniel Gilmore, "Another Brick in the Wall: Public Space, Visual Hegemonic Resistance, and the Physical/Digital Continuum," *Communication Theses*, paper 91 (MA thesis, Georgia State University, 2012).

4. Henrik Bjarneskans, Bjarne Grønnevik, and Anders Sandberg, "The Life-cycle of Memes" (1999), http://www.aleph.se/Trans/Cultural/Memetics/memecycle.html.

5. Alice Marwick and danah boyd, "I Tweet Honestly, I Tweet Passionately: Twitter Users, Context Collapse, and the Imagined Audience," *New Media and Society* 13 (2011): 96–113.

6. For more on attention economy, see Richard A. Lanham, *The Economics of Attention: Style and Substance in the Age of Information* (Chicago: University of Chicago Press, 2006).

7. Jean Burgess, "All Your Chocolate Rain Are Belong to Us? Viral Video, YouTube, and the Dynamics of Participatory Culture," in *Video Vortex Reader: Responses to YouTube*, ed. Geert Lovink and Sabine Niederer (Amsterdam: Institute of Network Cultures, 2008), 101–109.

Chapter 4

1. An elaborated account of the "mentalist approach," as well as a most illuminating discussion of memes, can be found in Daniel C. Dennett, *Darwin's Dangerous Idea: Evolution and the Meanings of Life* (New York: Touchstone, 1995).

2. For a detailed discussion of the "behavioral" approach, see Derek Gatherer, "Why the 'Thought Contagion' Metaphor Is Retarding the Progress of Memetics," *Journal of Memetics—Evolutionary Models of Information Transmission*, http://jom-emit.cfpm.org/1998/vol2/gatherer_d.html.

3. Patrick Davidson suggests using the dimension of "behavior" in addition to the dimensions of ideas and their expression. I think this dimension is particularly applicable to the analysis of genres, as I will outline in chapter 7. See Patrick Davidson, "The Language of (Internet) Memes," in *The Social Media Reader*, ed. Michael Mandiberg (New York: NYU Press, 2012), 120–127.

4. Susan U. Philips, "Participant Structures and Communicative Competence: Warm Springs Children in Community and Classroom," in *Functions of Language in the Classroom*, ed. Courtney B. Cazden, Vera P. John, and Dell H. Hymes (New York: Teachers College Press, 1972), 370–394; Shoshana

Blum-Kulka, Deborah Huck-Taglicht, and Hanna Avni, "The Social and Discursive Spectrum of Peer Talk," *Discourse Studies* 6, no. 3 (2004): 307–328, doi: 10.1177/1461445604044291; Roman Jakobson, "Linguistics and Poetics," in *Style in Language*, ed. Thomas A. Sebeok (Cambridge, MA: MIT Press, 1960), 350–377.

5. For further analysis of "Leave Britney Alone," see Aymar Jean Christian, "Camp 2.0: A Queer Performance of the Personal," *Communication, Culture, and Critique* 13, no. 3 (2010): 352–376; Nick Salvato, "Out of Hand: YouTube Amateurs and Professionals," *Drama Review* 53, no. 3 (2009): 67–83.

6. Noam Gal, "Internet Memes and the Construction of Collective Identity: The Case of 'It Gets Better'" (unpublished MA thesis, The Hebrew University of Jerusalem, 2012).

Chapter 5

1. Jeff Hemsley and Robert M. Mason, "The Nature of Knowledge in the Social Media Age: Implications for Knowledge Management Models," *Journal of Organizational Computing and Electronic Commerce* 23, no. 1–2 (2013):138–176.

2. Both types of videos can be relegated to what Jenkins et al. term *spreadable media* ("If It Doesn't Spread, It's Dead [Part One]: Media Viruses and Memes," Feb. 11, 2009, http://henryjenkins.org/2009/02/if_it_doesnt_spread_its_ dead_p.html). While I agree with Jenkins's criticism about the fuzziness of previous descriptions of viral media and Internet memes, I suggest that we should not abandon these terms, but rather attempt to define them better.

3. This does not mean that studies on this issue use only the word *viral*, but that this is a key term in this tradition. Prominent works that deal with the actors involved in online diffusion processes are Jure Leskovec, Lars Backstrom, and Jon Kleinberg, "Meme-Tracking and the Dynamics of the News Cycle," in *Proceedings of the 15th ACM SIGKDD International Conference on Knowledge Discovery and Data Mining* (Paris, June 28–July 1, 2009); and Gabe Ignatow and Alexander T. Williams, "New Media and the 'Anchor Baby' Boom," *Journal of Computer-Mediated Communication* 17, no. 1 (2011): 60.

4. Lada A. Adamic, Thomas M. Lento, and Andrew T. Fiore, "How You Met Me" (short paper, International AAAI Conference on Weblogs and Social Media, Dublin, June 4–7, 2012), http://www.aaai.org/ocs/index.php/ICWSM/ ICWSM12/paper/view/4681; Matthew P. Simmons, Lada A. Adamic, and Eytan Adar, "Memes Online: Extracted, Subtracted, Injected, and Recollected" (short paper, International AAAI Conference on Weblogs and Social Media,

Barcelona, July 17–21, 2011), http://www.aaai.org/ocs/index.php/ICWSM/ICWSM11/paper/view/2836/3281.

Chapter 6

1. Jonah Berger and Katherine Milkman, "What Makes Online Content Viral?," *Journal of Marketing Research*, 49 no. 2 (2012): 192–205.

2. For elaboration on the centrality of humor in "viral" circulation, see Joseph Phelps, Regina Lewis, Lynne Mobilio, David Perry, and Niranjan Raman, "Viral Marketing or Electronic Word-of-Mouth Advertising: Examining Consumer Responses and Motivations to Pass along Email," *Journal of Advertising Research 45*, no.4 (2004): 333–348; Guy Golan and Lior Zaidner, "Creative Strategies in Viral Advertising: An Application of Taylor's Six-Segment Message Strategy Wheel," *Journal of Computer-Mediated Communication*, 13, no. 4 (2008): 1083–6101.

3. Jenkins Blaise, "Consumer Sharing of Viral Video Advertisements: A Look into Message and Creative Strategy Typologies and Emotional Content: A Capstone Project" (MA thesis, American University, 2011), http://www.american.edu/soc/communication/upload/blaise-jenkins.pdf.

4. See Ethan Zuckerman's comprehensive blog post, "Unpacking Kony 2012," http://www.ethanzuckerman.com/blog/2012/03/08/unpacking-kony-2012/.

5. Ethan Zukerman, "Useful reads on Kony 2012," http://www.ethanzuckerman.com/blog/2012/03/14/useful-reads-on-kony-2012/.

6. Oliver Hinz, Bernd Skiera, Christian Barrot, and Jan Becker, "Seeding Strategies for Viral Marketing: An Empirical Comparison," *Journal of Marketing* 75, no. 6 (2011), http://www.marketingpower.com/AboutAMA/Documents/JM_Forthcoming/seeding_strategies_for_viral.pdf.

7. Gilad Lotan, "KONY2012: See How Invisible Networks Helped a Campaign Capture the World's Attention," http://blog.socialflow.com/post/7120244932/data-viz-kony2012-see-how-invisible-networks-helped-a-campaign-capture-the-worlds-attention.

8. Niklas Odén and Richard Larsson, "What Makes a Marketing Campaign a Viral Success? A Descriptive Model Exploring the Mechanisms of Viral Marketing," Umeå University, Faculty of Social Sciences, Department of Informatics, http://www.essays.se/essay/a028b08bc6/.

9. W. Lance Bennett and Alexandra Segerberg, "The Logic of Connective Action," *Information, Communication, and Society* 15, no. 5 (2012): 739–768.

10. Grant Meacham, "#Occupy: The Power of Revolution When It Becomes Memetic," Nov. 4, 2011, http://d-build.org/blog/?p=2995.

11. Limor Shifman, "An Anatomy of a YouTube Meme," *New Media and Society* 14, no. 2 (2012):187–203.

12. Jean Burgess and Joshua Green, *YouTube: Online Video and Participatory Culture* (Cambridge: Polity Press, 2009).

13. Colin Lankshear and Michele Knobel, *A New Literacies Sampler* (New York: Peter Lang, 2007).

14. Richard J. Pech, "Memes and Cognitive Hardwiring: Why Are Some Memes More Successful Than Others?," *European Journal of Innovation Management* 6, no. 3 (2003):173–181.

15. Henry Jenkins, Xiaochang Li, Ana Domb Krauskopf, and Joshua Green, "If It Doesn't Spread, It's Dead (Part One): Media Viruses and Memes," Feb. 11, 2009, http://henryjenkins.org/2009/02/if_it_doesnt_spread_its_dead_p.html.

16. John Fiske, *Television Culture* (London: Methuen, 1987).

Chapter 7

1. Wanda J. Orlikowski and JoAnne Yates, "Genre Repertoire: The Structuring of Communicative Practices in Organizations," *Administrative Science Quarterly* 39 (1994), 541–574.

2. Jean Elizabeth Burgess, "Vernacular Creativity and New Media" (PhD diss., Queensland University of Technology, Australia, 2007).

3. Ryan M. Milner, "The World Made Meme: Discourse and Identity in Participatory Media" (PhD diss., University of Kansas, 2012). Although meme creation has been simplified in the last decade, varying degrees of technological proficiency are applied for their creation: savvy Photoshoppers or editors "break the mold" more easily than others and thus stand out.

4. An illuminating analysis of Photoshop-based humor and the visual aspects underpinning Internet humor can be found in Giselinde Kuipers, "Media Culture and Internet Disaster Jokes: Bin Laden and the Attack on the World Trade Center," *European Journal of Cultural Studies* 5 (2002): 451–471.

5. Virág Molnár, "Reframing Public Space through Digital Mobilization: Flash Mobs and the Futility(?) of Contemporary Urban Youth Culture" (2009), http://www.scribd.com/doc/91277534/Reframing-Public-Space.

6. Joshua Walden, "Lip-sync in *Lipstick*: 1950s Popular Songs in a Television Series by Dennis Potter," *Journal of Musicological Research* 27 (2008): 169–195.

7. Dan Zak, "Office Drones, Lip-Sync Your Heart Out," *Washington Post*, Nov. 11, 2007, http://www.washingtonpost.com/wp-dyn/content/article/2007/11/08/AR2007110802060.html.

8. Graeme Turner, *Ordinary People and the Media* (London: Sage, 2009).

9. Lori Kendall, "Beyond Media Producers and Consumers: Online Multimedia Productions as Interpersonal Communication," *Information, Communication, and Society* 11, no. 2 (2008): 207–220.

10. Aaron Schwabach, "Reclaiming Copyright From the Outside In: What the Downfall Hitler Meme Means for Transformative Works, Fair Use, and Parody," *Buffalo Intellectual Property Law Journal* (2012), http://papers.ssrn.com/sol3/papers.cfm?abstract_id=2040538.

11. Kathleen Amy Williams, "Fake and Fan Film Trailers as Incarnations of Audience Anticipation and Desire, *Transformative Works and Cultures* 9 (2012), http://journal.transformativeworks.org/index.php/twc/article/view/360.

12. Ibid., 2.

13. Kate Miltner, "Srsly Phenomenal: An Investigation into the Appeal of LOL-Cats" (MA thesis, London School of Economics and Political Science, 2011).

14. Lee Knuttila, "User Unknowns: 4chan, Anonymity, and Contingency," *First Monday* 16, no. 10 (2012), http://firstmonday.org/htbin/cgiwrap/bin/ojs/index.php/fm/article/viewArticle/3665/3055.

15. Milner, "The World Made Meme," 66.

16. Ibid., 70.

Chapter 8

1. Limor Shifman, Stephen Coleman, and Stephen Ward, "Only Joking? Online Humour in the 2005 UK General Election," *Information, Communication, and Society*, 10, no. 4 (2007): 465–487.

2. On the role of new media in these protests, see Zeynep Tufekci and Christopher Wilson, "Social Media and the Decision to Participate in Political Protest: Observations from Tahrir Square," *Journal of Communication* 62, no. 12 (2012): 363–379; Gilad Lotan, Erhardt Graeff, Mike Ananny, Devin Gaffney, Ian Pearce, and danah boyd, "The Revolutions Were Tweeted: Information Flows During the 2011 Tunisian and Egyptian Revolutions," *International*

Journal of Communication 5 (2012): 1375–1405. A critical analysis of the role of new media in these protests can be found in Gadi Wolfsfeld, Tamir Sheafer, and Elad Segev, "The Social Media and the Arab Spring: Politics Always Comes First," *International Journal of Press/Politics* 18, no. 2 (2013): 115–137.

3. W. Lance Bennett and Alexandra Segerberg, "The Logic of Connective Action," *Information, Communication, and Society* 15, no. 5 (2012): 739–768.

4. Ryan Milner, "The World Made Meme: Discourse and Identity in Participatory Media" (PhD diss., University of Kansas, 2012).

5. Elihu Katz and Paul Lazarsfeld, *Personal Influence* (Glencoe, IL: Free Press of Glencoe, 1955).

6. Travis Ridout, Erika Franklin Fowler, and John Branstetter, "Political Advertising in the 21st Century: The Rise of the YouTube Ad" (paper presented at the annual meeting of the American Political Science Association, Washington, DC, September 2–5, 2010), http://papers.ssrn.com/sol3/papers.cfm?abstract_id=1642853.

7. Kevin Wallsten, "Yes We Can: How Online Viewership, Blog Discussion, Campaign Statements, and Mainstream Media Coverage Produced a Viral Video Phenomenon," *Journal of Information, Technology, and Politics* 7, nos. 2–3 (2010): 163–181.

8. Karine Nahon, Jeff Hemsley, Shawn Walker, and Muzammil Hussain, "Fifteen Minutes of Fame: The Place of Blogs in the Life Cycle of Viral Political Information," *Policy and Internet* 3, no. 1 (2011).

9. Bennett and Segerberg, "The Logic of Connective Action."

10. Nathan Schneider, "From Occupy Wall Street to Occupy Everywhere," *Nation*, October 31, 2011.

11. Geniesa Tay, "Embracing LOLitics: Popular Culture, Online Political Humor, and Play" (MA thesis, University of Canterbury, 2012).

12. Erving Goffman, *The Presentation of Self in Everyday Life* (New York: Doubleday, 1959).

13. On various forms of scandals and talk scandals, see John B. Thompson, *Political Scandal: Power and Visibility in the Media Age* (Cambridge: Polity, 2000); Mats Ekstrom and Bengt Johansson, "Talk Scandals," *Media, Culture, and Society* 30, no. 1 (2008): 61–79.

14. Jonathan Alan Gray, Jeffrey P. Jones, and Ethan Thompson, "The State of Satire, the Satire of State," in *Satire TV: Politics and Comedy in the Post-Network*

Era, ed. Jonathan Alan Gray, Jeffrey Jones, and Ethan Thompson (New York: NYU Press, 2009), 3–36.

15. Henry Jenkins, *Convergence Culture: Where Old and New Media Collide* (New York: NYU Press, 2008).

16. Christopher Rea, "Spoofing (*e'gao*) Culture on the Chinese Internet," in *Humor in Chinese Life and Letters: Modern and Contemporary Approaches*, ed. Jessica Milner Davis and Jocelyn Chey (Hong Kong: Hong Kong University Press, forthcoming).

17. Jiang Zemin, cited in Xi Chen, "Dynamics of News Media Regulations in China: Explanations and Implications," *Journal of Comparative Asian Development* 5 (2006): 49–64.

18. Rea, "Spoofing (*e'gao*) Culture on the Chinese Internet."

19. Shaojung Sharon Wang, "China's Internet Lexicon: The Symbolic Meaning and Commoditization of Grass Mud Horse in the Harmonious Society," *First Monday* 17, nos. 1–2 (2012), http://www.firstmonday.org/htbin/cgiwrap/bin/ojs/index.php/fm/article/view/3758/3134.

20. Ibid.

21. Lillian Boxman-Shabtai, "Ethnic Humor in the Digital Age: A Reevaluation" (MA thesis, Hebrew University of Jerusalem, 2012).

Chapter 9

1. John Tomlinson, *Cultural Imperialism: A Critical Introduction* (London: Pinter, 1991).

2. Shani Orgad, "The Cultural Dimensions of Online Communication: A Study of Breast Cancer Patients' Internet Spaces," *New Media and Society* 8, no. 6 (2006): 877–899; Charles Ess and Fay Sudweeks, "Culture and Computer-Mediated Communication: Toward New Understanding," *Journal of Computer Mediated Communication* 11, no. 1, article 9 (2005), http://jcmc.indiana.edu/vol11/issue1/ess.html.

3. Roland Robertson, "Glocalization: Time-Space and Homogeneity-Heterogeneity," in *Global Modernities*, ed. Mike Featherstone, Scott Lash, and Roland Robertson (London: Sage, 1995), 25–44, 28.

4. Robert McChesney, "So Much for the Magic of Technology and the Free Market: The World Wide Web and the Corporate Media System," in *The World Wide Web and Contemporary Cultural Theory*, ed. Andrew Herman and Thomas

Swiss (London: Routledge, 2000), 5–35; N. A. John, "The Construction of the Multilingual Internet: Unicode, Hebrew, and Globalization," *Journal of Computer-Mediated Communication* 18 (2013) 321–338.

5. David Crystal, "The Future of Englishes," in *Analyzing English in a Global Context*, ed. Ann Burns and Caroline Coffin (London: Routledge, 2001), 53–64.

6. Limor Shifman and Mike Thelwall, "Assessing Global Diffusion with Web Memetics: The Spread and Evolution of a Popular Joke," *Journal of the American Society for Information Science and Technology* 60, no. 12 (2009): 2567–2576.

7. For elaboration on Internet-based "Mars and Venus" humor, see Limor Shifman and Dafna Lemish, "'Mars and Venus' in Virtual Space: Post-feminist Humor and the Internet," *Critical Studies in Media Communication* 28, no. 3 (2011): 253–273; Limor Shifman and Dafna Lemish, "Between Feminism and Fun(ny) mism: Analyzing Gender in Popular Internet Humor," *Information, Communication, and Society* 13, no. 6 (2010): 870–891.

8. Limor Shifman, Hadar Levy, and Mike Thelwall, "Internet Memes as Globalizing Agents?" (paper presented at the Association of Internet Researchers [AoIR] 13th Conference, Salford, England, October 2012).

9. On humor as based on opposing scripts, see Victor Raskin, *Semantic Mechanisms of Humor* (Dordrecht: Reidel, 1985).

10. Ryan Milner, "The World Made Meme: Discourse and Identity in Participatory Media" (PhD diss., University of Kansas, 2012), 179–182.

11. Penelope Eckert, "The Meaning of Style," in *SALSA XI: Proceedings of the Eleventh Annual Symposium about Language and Society*, ed. Wai Fong Chiang, Elaine Chun, Laura Mahalingappa, and Siri Mehus (Austin: Texas Linguistics Forum, 2004).

12. See http://english.alarabiya.net/articles/2012/11/04/247600.html.

Chapter 10

1. Ryan Milner, "The World Made Meme: Discourse and Identity in Participatory Media" (PhD diss., University of Kansas, 2012).

2. Asaf Nissenboim, "Lurk More, It's Never Enough: Memes as Social Capital on 4chan" (MA thesis, Hebrew University of Jerusalem, in progress).

FURTHER READINGS

Aunger, Robert, ed. *Darwinizing Culture: The Status of Memetics as a Science*. Oxford: Oxford University Press, 2000.

Blackmore, Susan. *The Meme Machine*. Oxford: Oxford University Press, 1999.

Burgess, Jean, and Joshua Green. *YouTube: Online Video and Participatory Culture*. Malden, MA: Polity, 2009.

Coleman, Gabriella. *Coding Freedom: The Ethics and Aesthetics of Hacking*. Princeton: Princeton University Press, 2012.

Dawkins, Richard. *The Selfish Gene*. Oxford: Oxford University Press, 1976.

Dennett, Daniel C. *Darwin's Dangerous Idea: Evolution and the Meanings of Life*. New York: Touchstone, 1995.

Jenkins, Henry. *Convergence Culture: Where Old and New Media Collide*. New York: NYU Press, 2006.

Jenkins, Henry, Sam Ford, and Joshua Green. *Spreadable Media: Creating Value and Meaning in a Networked Culture*. New York: NYU Press, 2013.

Lanham, Richard A. *The Economics of Attention: Style and Substance in the Age of Information*. Chicago: University of Chicago Press, 2006.

Lankshear, Colin, and Michele Knobel. *A New Literacies Sampler*. New York: Peter Lang, 2007.

Milner, Ryan M. The world made meme: Discourse and identity in participatory media. PhD diss., University of Kansas, 2012.

INDEX

Note: Page numbers in italic type indicate illustrations.

in political memes, 134
Owling, 103

Packaging, 69, 94, 96. *See also*
    Repackaging
"Paper Planes," 76
Parodies, 46–48
Participation, virality dependent on,
    72–73, 94, 96. *See also* Political
    participation
Participation structures, 40, 44
Participatory culture. *See also* Web
    2.0
    characteristics of, 4, 18
    incompleteness as invitation to,
        86, 88, 94
    political participation on Internet,
        120, 122
    as subject and agent of memetic
        videos, 89
"Peanut Butter Jelly Time," 74,
    82–83
Pennies from Heaven (television
    series), 105
"Pepper-Spraying Cop," 50–51, *52*,
    53, 58, 92
Personalized content sharing,
    72–73
Personal webcams, 105
Persuasion, 122–127
Phatic communication, 41, 45
Phelps, Joseph, 61, 67
Phenotypes, 38
Phillips, Susan, 40
Phonetic translation, 108–109
Photo fads, 102–103
Photographs. *See* Memetic photos
Photoshop, 2, 15, 22, 51, 89, 90,
    100, 102, 143, 150

Pike, John, 50–51, 92
Planking, 28, 29, 30, 103
Plato, 81
Playfulness, 79, 84
Poetic communication, 41
"Poker Face," 115
Political jokes, 149–150
Political memes, 119–150
    as action, 123, 127–138
    critical use of, 141, 143–149
    as democratic subversion, 144–149
    as discourse, 123, 127–138, 150
    functions of, 122–123
    as persuasion, 122–127
    photos as, 138–144
    political participation through, 72,
        120, 122, 144
    popular culture in, 136, 138
Political participation, 72, 120, 122,
    144
Politics
    as content, 51, 79, 119–150
    Internet memes' impact on, 174
    of memetic activities, 172–173
    scandals in, 140
Polysemy, 150
Popular culture
    audiences' relationship with, 110
    memes based on, 51
    in memetic videos, 84
    in political memes, 136, 138
Positioning, 70–71, 96
Positivity, 66–67, 94
Postmodernism, 15
Potter, Dennis, 105
Presidential campaigns
    2008, 120, 122, 124–127
    2012, 4, 168
Prestige, 69–70, 96